REASON
TO
BELIEVE

A Response to Common Objections to Christianity

R.C. Sproul

Foreword by
Lee Strobel

ZondervanPublishingHouse
Grand Rapids, Michigan

A Division of HarperCollins*Publishers*

To Archie Parrish
for his unceasing labor and personal devotion
to the proclamation
of the Lordship of Jesus Christ.

Reason To Believe
Copyright © 1978 by G/L Publications
All rights reserved

First Zondervan Printing 1982

Requests for information should be addressed to:
Zondervan Publishing House
Grand Rapids, Michigan 49530

Library of Congress Cataloging-in-Publication Data

Sproul, R. C. (Robert Charles), 1939-
    Reason to Believe.
    Reprint. Originally published: Objections answered. Gospel Light, 1978.
    Bibliography: p.
    1. Apologetics—20th century.   I. Title.
  BT1102.S59   239   81-21900
  ISBN 0-310-44911-1   AACR2

Printed in the United States of America

Cover design by Jerry Fahselt
Cover illustration by Jerry Fahselt

00 01 02 /DC/ 41 40 39 38 37 36 35 34 33 32 31

contents

Is the Bible Full of Myths?/ Does the Bible Conflict with Science?/ Is the Bible Filled with Contradictions?/ Is the Bible Inaccurate Historically? / Why Is Some of the Bible Offensive?/ Are Scriptures Infallible?/ Key Points to Remember

Aren't All Religions Basically the Same?/ Why Is God So Narrow-Minded?/ Why Do Christians Say that Christ Is God Incarnate?/ Key Points to Remember

foreword

I'll admit it: I was a spiritual skeptic for much of my life.

I thought Christians were gullible people who had fallen prey to their own wishful thinking. Had not Freud and Marx and Darwin successfully dismantled the foundation of Christianity? Certainly if Christians could learn to apply a little common sense, they would see that their faith is riddled with irrationality.

Or so I thought.

Then I was prompted by my wife's conversion to begin checking out Christianity in a systematic way. I used my journalistic and legal training to investigate whether there was, indeed, any truth to the Christian claims.

This book, under an earlier title, was one of the first I read, and it stunned me. It provided reasoned responses to some of the exact objections I was raising. And it defended the Christian faith with a compelling logic that helped destroy my image of Christians as being intellectual weaklings. In a very real sense, God used it to propel me toward the truth about Him.

Today I am a follower of Jesus Christ. In my role as an evangelist I often give skeptics this same book. "Take a look at this," I tell them, "and then let's talk." I also recommend the book to Christians, saying, "Here is a great way to follow 1 Peter 3:15 by preparing yourself to respond to questions about the faith."

Years after I became a Christian, I had an opportunity to meet R. C. Sproul, and I wholeheartedly thanked him for writing such a powerful and persuasive book. And I believe that after you read *Reason to Believe*—whether you are a spiritual skeptic whose questions are keeping you from God or a Christian who wants to prepare yourself for evangelistic encounters— you are going to want to thank him, too.

Lee Strobel
Willow Creek Community Church
September 1993

preface

The Christian faith has never been without its critics. Criticisms from every source have been leveled against Christianity since its inception. It is remarkable that after experiencing almost 2,000 years of such criticism the Christian faith continues to thrive as a viable life and world view. Philosophies and alternate religious systems that have sought to supplant Christianity have come and gone. Current philosophical "isms" tend to have a very short life span. Yet classic objections to Christianity continue to be raised. Some of the objections are raised in a spirit of prejudice and hostility. Others are raised out of a genuine attempt to resolve very perplexing issues and mysteries.

The purpose of this book is not to provide a technical study in the science of apologetics, which science is designed to give a comprehensive defense of the intellectual credibility of Christianity. Rather this book is designed for laymen; to offer basic answers to the most common and frequent objections that are raised about Christianity. This book treats matters that range from such philosophical questions as the problem of evil to the very practical and personal frustrations that people encounter when confronted by hypocrisy. Ultimately it is the hope of the author that students and critics of the Christian faith would direct their attention to the Scriptures of the Old and New Testaments in a serious attempt to discover answers within its pages to the questions of life.

I hope this book will serve as an introduction and springboard to more in-depth examinations of the problems that are discussed. The Christian must always be prepared to give honest answers to honest questions. Flights into private preference of belief or irrational assertions of dogmatism bring no honor to Christ. It is our responsibility "to give a reason for the hope that lies within us." (See 1 Pet. 3:15.)

R.C. Sproul

acknowledgements

Special thanks are offered to the man to whom this book is dedicated, Archie Parrish. It was out of his concern to answer questions people raised in discussion about the Christian faith that this work was prompted. Through his ministry of training laymen for evangelism the need for such a basic training guide was established. The list of questions dealt with have been supplied by laymen involved with Mr. Parrish's ministry. I particularly hope that these laymen will find thisvolume helpful.

I must express gratitude for the assistance rendered by Mr. Stuart Boehmig, Mrs. Alane Barron, and Miss Mary Semach who helped with the preparation of the manuscript.

introduction
A Personal Pilgrimage

The quest for the meaning of life was a troublesome problem for me from an early age. The "why" questions were the ones that gripped my mind—not so much physical questions but metaphysical questions. Many children are fascinated by "how" things work. They may even pester their parents with questions like, What makes a car run? How does a clock work? How does a seed turn into a flower? I had childhood friends like that, forever tinkering with cars and lawnmowers and skeletons. Some became engineers, some doctors, one a geologist and one a physicist. But I was bored with those questions. I knew they were very important questions, but they simply were not the ones on my mind.

As a youth I had two consuming passions. One was

sports and the other the "why" questions. I saw no relationship between them at the time but in present reflection I think I can see how they fit together in my own circumstances.

I was a wartime child. The earliest question that plagued me was the question of war. I wanted to know why there were wars. They seemed pretty silly to me at age four. I couldn't understand why Roosevelt and Hitler couldn't sit at a table and resolve their differences without using tanks and bombs and ships. Of course I had a personal vested interest in the question. What the war meant to me personally was the absence of my father. From age two to age six my father was a picture of a man in uniform. He was the one who wrote air letters to us. He was the one my mother talked about and typed letters to every night. She let me punch the X and O keys at the end of every letter. For some strange reason none of my childhood friends' fathers were away at war. I kept wondering, "Why does everyone else have a dad at home and I don't?"

The plaguing question of war evaporated for me with a happy ending. Playing stickball on the streets of Chicago I was startled by the sound of people screaming and beating on pots and pans. I watched them hug each other and behave in a very strange manner. I was upset that their antics interrupted the stickball game until I understood what it was all about—V.J. Day, 1945.

The full implications of their jubilation did not hit me until I stood in a railroad terminal that looked as if it was filled with a million men in uniform and a lot of weeping women. Then the troop trains came in. In the midst of a multitude of soldiers who all looked the same, one of them caught my eye. Fifty feet away he dropped his duffle bag, dropped to his knees and threw open his arms with a flashing grin on his face. I broke from my mother's hand and covered the fifty feet in Guinness record time. Dodging servicemen and running around duffle bags I flew into the arms of my father. The war didn't matter anymore.

Then came school. From day one I didn't like school. It is still something of a mystery to me how I ever ended up in an academic vocation. I remember walking to school on Mondays dreaming about Fridays. The thought that plagued me was why do I have to go to school five days a week and get to play only two? It didn't make sense to me. My father's schedule looked even worse. It seemed like he was always working. I wondered what life was all about when you had to spend so much time doing what you don't like so you could spend so little time doing what you do like.

I was a good student but my heart wasn't in it. Sports were my passion. Sports made sense to me. I took a sensuous and intellectual pleasure in them. I liked the feel of my body responding to action moves: dodging a would-be tackler, driving through the key for an "un-makeable" lay-up; skirting across the bag at second and firing to first for a double play. I was consumed by sports. I read every book in our school and town library on sports. I was a walking encyclopedia of sports "trivia." My hero was the fictional Chip Hilton. He excelled at everything; he was a pristine model of fair play; he was a champion.

Practice for sports was never work. I was never so tired that I wanted practice to end. I loved every second of it. There was a reason for practice. The game. Victory. The game had a starting point, a goal, and an end point. Victory was a real possibility; defeat never entered my mind. When we were behind my thoughts were never "What if we lose?" but rather, "How can we win?" Like Vince Lombardi, I never lost a game but just ran out of time on a few occasions. My coaches were my real-life idols because they always pointed ways to victory. We would be willing to die for them on the field as a matter of obvious course.

But something happened that changed all that and changed me so radically that I'm not over it yet. I was 16 years old when my mother came to me and said, "Son, your father has an incurable disease. There is nothing the doctors can do for him. You can still play some sports but you'll have to cut back and get a part-time job. Dad is dying and you have to be the man of the house." I took the message outwardly with stoic heroism. Inwardly I was enraged. I could not believe there was such a thing as an unsolvable problem. We won the war, didn't we? We always found a way to win ball games. Why can't we beat this? There must be a cure. The doctors are wrong. But there was no cure. The doctors were right. Dad didn't die right away. He died a day at a time. Every night I fireman-dragged his emaciated body to the dinner table.

I still played sports for a while but it was different. They were foolishness. The coach said, "Sproul, I want you to take this football and carry it with you everywhere you go. I want you to take it to dinner and sleep with it. You have to eat, drink, and sleep football."

Two weeks earlier if he had said that to me I would have loved him for it. Now I wanted to scream at him, "You idiot! Don't you know this stuff doesn't matter at all!" Practice was misery. The games became a nightmare. Sports, like life, were an exercise in futility. Chip Hilton was a myth and life a bitter joke. When the referee blew his whistle and called a foul I pushed his whistle in his mouth. When the umpire called me out I took a swing at him. Bitter, frustrated, confused, I knew only defeat. Now there was no way to win. I quit.

The last time my father fell I picked him up and carried him to bed, unconscious. Twenty hours later he was dead. No tears from me—no emotion. I "quarterbacked" the funeral arrangements. When we put him in the ground my soul went under with him. The next year was a year of unrestrained degeneracy. (Anger can do a lot of things to a young man.) I became the paradigm of the angry young man. In junior high I graduated second in my class, legitimately; from senior high I was one hundred fifty-seventh by every crooked means available.

Sandlot football won me a scholarship to college. Then came radicalizing number two. One week on campus and my life was turned upside down again. The star of the football team called me aside and told me about Jesus. I couldn't believe this guy. In my eyes ministers were "pansies," and "Christian" was a synonym for "sissy." I don't remember what he said to me; but it drove me to the New Testament. Truth breathed from every page. It was my virgin experience with the Bible. It was a spiritual experience of revolution. I always knew there was a God but I hated Him. In this week my anger and bitterness dissolved into repentance. The result was forgiveness and life.

It would perhaps be appropriate to relate a story of coming to Christ via the route of intellectual inquiry. But that's not how it happened with me. The intellectual drive came later. For one year I had a consummate passion to learn the Scriptures. I couldn't understand why everyone didn't believe them. Most of my professors were skeptics. The campus atmosphere was mostly secular. I was quickly faced with every conceivable intellectual objection to Christianity. I was most vulnerable, in light of my past history, to the charge that my faith grew out of my emotional trauma and psychological need for Jesus to be my "Father" and to give me hope in my despair and bitterness.

I wasn't a Christian long until I had to face the question squarely: Was my conversion rooted in objective reality or was it merely an expression of my own subjective needs? I began to experience what Saint Augustine called, "Faith seeking understanding." Thus I turned my attention to the study of philosophy as my major academic pursuit.

The study of the history of philosophy exposed me to virtually every serious alternative to Christianity the world has brought forth. I began to see the bankruptcy of secular world views. I found valuable insights in Spinoza, Kant, Sartre, and others. But no one seemed to have a consistent and coherent life and world view. The philosophers themselves were their own best critics. Hume critiqued Locke; Kant critiqued Hume; Hegel critiqued Kant, and so on it went. There emerged no "sure results" of speculative thought. The study of philosophy did provide very important tools for critical analysis which have proved very helpful for my own pilgrimage. The more I studied philosophy the more intellectually credible and satisfying Christianity became.

After college came seminary. Naively I expected seminary to be a citadel of scholarly interpretation and defense of Christianity. Instead I found it to be a fortress of skepticism and unbelief. A negative posture toward classical Christianity prevailed which exposed me to a wide variety of contemporary critical theories that rejected orthodox Christianity. Thus seminary exposed me to a wide variety of scholarly criticisms of the Bible. This forced me to face the question of the trustworthiness of Scripture. Fortunately I was blessed with two crucial support systems. On the one hand I was well-enough equipped with the tools of analytical philosophy to spot the philosophical assumptions that the negative critics were using. Through philosophical tools I was able, to some degree, to critique the critics. I was intellectually unimpressed by the weak philosophical assumptions of the "liberal" professors. On the other hand I was fortunate to study under one professor who did affirm classical Christianity. He was our toughest professor and most academically demanding. His "bear-trap" mind and singular ability for "close" and "tight" reasoning impressed me. He seemed to tower over the rest of the professors both in knowledge and analytical brilliance.

From seminary I went on to a doctoral program in Europe. It was a difficult and exhilarating experience. Almost all of my work had to be done in foreign languages which required a new kind of intellectual discipline for me. Studying under G.C. Berkouwer of the Free University of Amsterdam exposed me to all the latest theories of theology and biblical studies. The European system exposed me to the method of approaching theology and biblical studies as a technical science. Studying the primary sources in original languages such as Dutch, German and Latin gave me new tools for scholarship.

From Europe I returned to America and began my teaching career. Teaching in both college and seminary I had an unusual pattern of teaching assignments. At one college I taught almost exclusively in the field of philosophy. In another college I was responsible to teach theology and biblical studies. My first seminary appointment had me teaching philosophical theology which combined both philosophy and theology. Oddly enough I was also asked to teach New Testament theology. In an age of specialization I was forced into being a "generalist," working in several different but related fields.

The science of apologetics which offers intellectual defense of the credibility of Christianity finally became my point of "specialty." That is usually what happens to generalists.

My training was not in a conservative "hothouse." I have been through the gamut of liberal scholarship. I am a first-generation conservative—by conviction, not heritage or training.

The teaching arena has been the crucible of my thinking. The more I study and the more I teach and engage in dialogue with unbelievers and critics the more confident I have become in the rock-solid intellectual integrity and truth of Christianity. In fact, I am overwhelmed by the profundity, coherency, and intricate internal consistency of Christianity. I am awed by the majesty and brilliance, not to mention the power, of the Scriptures. Take away the Scriptures and you take away Christ. Take away Christ and you take away life. My conviction is one with that of Luther: *Spiritus Sanctus non est scepticus:* "The Holy Spirit is not a skeptic and the assertions He has given us are surer and more certain than sense and life itself."

one

"The Bible Contradicts Itself. It's Just a Fairy Tale."

Christians, to support their claim of revealed truth, appeal to a book that was written hundreds of years ago. This book—the Bible—has been a subject of an enormous amount of study and criticism which has left the integrity of its trustworthiness seriously in doubt. If the Bible were universally regarded as an authoritarian source book for religious truth, many of the questions we will deal with in *Reason to Believe* would be easily resolved. But the authority and trustworthiness of the Bible is presently in question.

It is well beyond the scope of this book to give a comprehensive defense of the integrity of Scripture. Such a comprehensive defense would involve so many complex matters that it deserves separate treatment. A large number of such works have been published in recent years.[1]

But, several common questions about the integrity of Scripture are dealt with briefly here.

Is the Bible Full of Myths?

That the Bible is a book of myths is a common charge leveled by its critics. Since myths have no counterpart in historical truth, they are considered to be worthless sources of truth. One dictionary definition of myth terms it as "any fictitious story."

Why is it so often said that the Bible is full of myths? A chief reason is because of the numerous accounts of miracles that are found in its pages. Another reason is because of parallel accounts between such things as the biblical view of the flood and that found, for example, in Babylonian mythology. A third reason why the presence of myth is suspected is because there exist similarities between events surrounding Jesus and portraits of the gods found in Greek mythology. These three reasons serve as the substantial basis for attributing a mythological character to biblical literature.

A question of miracle is not merely a question of literary style but it involves important questions of history and philosophy. If a miracle is rejected as a myth because the critic assumes that miracles cannot happen, then the issue becomes one of the philosophy of nature and history rather than one of literary analysis. Before miracles can be rejected out of hand as *ipso facto* impossible, the critic must first establish that we are living in a closed mechanistic universe in which there exists no possibility of divine or supernatural intrusion. On the other hand, if there is a God who is omnipotent, then miracles are possible and accounts of them cannot be gratuitously dismissed as myths.

If we allow that miracles are possible that does not mean that every claim to them is valid. It is one thing to say that miracles could have happened; it is quite another to say that they did happen. As we deal with the question of an alleged miracle we must deal with it not only on the grounds of the possibility, but on the evidence that is offered to support its claim.

One of the interesting elements of biblical miracles involves the sobriety of their accounts. Compare, for example, miracle narratives of the New Testament with those found in the Gnostic literature of the second century. The Gnostic "miracles" display a flavor and atmosphere of the bizarre and frivolous. New Testament miracles take place in a context of a sober view of history and redemption. Those who claim them are men of obvious profound ethical integrity and men who are willing to die for their veracity. When evaluating the claims of biblical miracles it is important to understand the total value system of those who are making the claims. The biblical writers, in the Judeo-Christian tradition, write with a constraint that involves a profound commitment to the sanctity of truth. Peter, for example, argues, "We do not declare unto you cleverly devised myths or fables but rather what we have seen with our eyes and heard with our ears" (see 2 Pet. 1:16).

Because there are parallel accounts of ancient events found in the Bible as well as in ancient mythological literature, this is no justification for impugning the writers of Scripture on the basis of the fallacy of guilt by association. If we assume, for example, that there was a natural catastrophe such as a flood in the ancient world, it should not surprise us that the event is reflected in the writings of other ancient people. The Christian welcomes a close study of comparison between the biblical account of the flood and that found, for example, in the

Gilgamish Epic.[2] That the biblical account is already demythologized appears self-evident.

The charge that the New Testament surrounds the person of Christ with mythology is often inferred from similarities of dying and rising gods in Greek mythology such as are found in Ovid's *Metamorphoses*. However, in a comparative examination of any object or event under analysis the scientific method demands that we note not only the similarities but the differences as well. Mythic creatures that are half man and half beast, for example, are noticeably absent from the Scriptures. Bizarre stories about the creation of the universe are also conspicuously absent. The world, for example, is nowhere described in Scriptures as an appendage of a god; nor do we see notions of the world coming into being as the result of sexual acts of procreation among the gods. Though Jesus is virgin born, He does not spring anew out of the head of Zeus.

At the heart of the difference between Greek mythology and biblical literature is a radically different view of the significance of history. For the Greek there is no overt attempt to ground myth within the framework of history. Indeed, for the gods to become actually incarnate in the realm of space and time is utterly repugnant to the Greek mind. On the other hand that which is non-historical or anti-historical is relegated to the level of falsehood by the Hebrew. This radically opposing view of history is essential to understanding the Jewish-Greek antithesis with respect to the question of myth.

Does the Bible Conflict with Science?

Perhaps nothing has contributed more to the loss of credibility of Scripture than the conflicts between religion and science that have come out of the scientific and technological revolution. We remember the condemnation of Galileo and the circus atmosphere of the Scopes "Monkey Trials." Galileo was condemned for teaching that the sun was the center of our solar system (heliocentricity) over against the accepted view that the earth was the center (geocentricity). The bishops of the church in Galileo's day refused to look into his telescope and examine the empirical evidence that the earth is not the center of our solar system. The church is still feeling the embarrassment of that episode.

Some argue that the Bible teaches a view of reality that is utterly in conflict with the assured results of modern scientific inquiry. Some allege that the Bible teaches a primitive, prescientific view of the universe which is no longer tenable to modern man. The Bible describes the universe as being "three-storied" with heaven above, the earth in the middle, and hell underneath the earth. It describes a world of demons and angels which is considered in conflict with modern theories of physics and biology.

How does the Christian respond to such allegations? In the first place, it must be acknowledged that the church indeed has made grievous errors in drawing scientific inferences from the Scriptures that were unwarranted. Nowhere does the Bible "teach" that the earth is the center of the universe. The Scripture describes nature from a phenomenological perspective. That is, the world of nature is described as it appears to the naked eye. The sun is described as moving across the heavens. The Bible speaks of sunrises and sunsets. And in popular speech modern scientists still speak in the same manner. One needs only to observe the daily weather forecast to see this taking place. The weather report, or "meteorological" survey, is couched in technical scientific jargon. We hear about high pressure systems, barometric pressure, precipitation probability quotients, and the like. Yet at the end of the forecast we are told that the sun will rise at a given time and will set at another time. We do not phone the news station and angrily demand that such antiquated notions of geocentricity be deleted from the weather forecast. We do not charge the scientists with being unscientific when they describe things phenomenologically. We shouldn't do that to the biblical writers either.

That the Bible speaks of a demonic world is evident. The Bible does not, however, teach that diseases and other mysterious maladies are caused by demonic activity. The Scriptures recognize and endorse the practice of medicine. I might add that the notion of the existence of a demonic world conflicts with no known natural scientific law.

The Bible is not a textbook of science. It does not purport to instruct us in matters of calculus, physics, or chemistry. There are times, however, when serious conflicts do emerge between theories inferred from science and biblical teaching. If, for example, a scientist concludes that the origin of man is a cosmic accident, then the scientist holds a position that is antithetical to the teaching of Scripture. But the question of man's origin can never be determined by the study of biology. The question of origin is a question of history. The biologist can describe how things *could have* happened, but can never tell us how they did happen.

Is the Bible Filled with Contradictions?

People accept without hesitation the charge that the Bible is full of contradictions. Yet the charge is completely inaccurate and misleading. Why, then, if the charge is so inaccurate, do we hear it so often repeated? Apart from the problem of prejudice, there are other reasons why this misconception is propagated. There is a problem not only of ignorance of what the Bible says, but perhaps even more so, a problem of ignorance of the laws of logic. The word "contradiction" is used all too loosely with respect to biblical content. That there are divergencies of biblical accounts, that biblical writers describe the same things from different perspectives, is not in dispute. Whether those varied accounts are, in fact, contradictory is in dispute.

It would be a serious overstatement to say that all discrepancies within the biblical text have been easily and satisfactorily resolved. There are serious discrepancies that have not yielded full and satisfactory resolutions. But these problems are few and far between. To say that the Bible is full of contradictions is a radical exaggeration and reflects a misunderstanding of the law of contradiction. For example, critics have alleged repeatedly that the Gospel writers contradict each other with respect to the number of angels present at the tomb of Jesus. One writer mentions one angel and the other writer mentions two angels. However, the writer who mentions one angel does not say there was *only* one angel. He merely speaks of one angel. Now if in fact there were two angels, it is mathematically certain that there was also one angel. There is no contradiction in that. Now, if one writer said there was only one angel and the other writer said there were two, at the same time and in the same relationship, there would be a bonafide contradiction.

The problem of the loose use of the word contradiction came home to me in a discussion I had with a seminary student. He repeated the charge, "The Bible is full of contradictions." I said to him, "The Bible is a large book. If it is full of contradictions you should have no problem finding 50 clear violations of the law of contradiction in the next 24 hours. Why don't you go home and write down 50 contradictions and we'll discuss them at the same time tomorrow." He accepted the challenge.

The next day he returned bleary-eyed with a list of 30 contradictions. He admitted that he had worked long into the night and could come up with only 30. But he presented me a list of the most blatant contradictions he could find. (He made use of critical books that listed such contradictions.) He went through his list, one at a time, applying the test of formal logic to each alleged contradiction. We used syllogisms, the laws of immediate inference, truth tables, and even Venn diagrams to test for logical inconsistency and contradictions. In every single incident we proved objectively, not only to my satisfaction, but to his, that not a single violation of the law of contradiction was made.

Not every biblical discrepancy has been resolved. But the direction of the evidence is very encouraging. As biblical scholarship increases and our knowledge of language, text, and context increases, the problem of discrepancy becomes smaller and smaller. There is less reason today to believe that the Bible is full of contradictions than at any time in the history of the church. Prejudice and critical philosophical theories, however, die a very slow and hard death.

Is the Bible Inaccurate Historically?

If any area of biblical scholarship has given us reason for optimism concerning the reliability of Scripture, it is the area of historical investigation. To be sure there are certain dimensions of biblical content that are difficult to either verify or falsify by means of historical research. For example, the existence of angels can hardly be verified through archeological research. Unless we can dig up some petrified angel wings we must deal with these matters on other grounds. But where biblical material touches on areas where historical research is possible it has come out remarkably well.

Twentieth-century discoveries such as those at Ugarit, Qumran and Ebla have done much to enhance our understanding of antiquity. The Nuzi tablets and the Armana tablets have resolved a host of Old Testament problems. The work of Ramsey tracing the journeys of Paul as recorded by Luke has so vindicated Luke's accuracy as a historian, that modern secular historians have called him the finest historian of antiquity. The biblical historians have fared considerably better under close scrutiny and critique than have other ancient historians such as Josephus and Herodotus.

The Christian has nothing to fear from rigorous historical research. Rather, we have everything to gain. To illustrate the weight of historical research let us note one of the last statements made in print by the dean of archeological scholarship in the twentieth century, Dr. William Foxwell Albright:

> For much too long a time the course of New Testament scholarship has been dictated by theological, quasitheological, and philosophical presupposition. In far too many cases commentaries on New Testament books have neglected such basic requirements as up-to-date historical and philological analysis of the text itself. In many ways this preoccupation with theological and metaphysical interpretation is the unacknowledged child of Hegelianism. To this should be added the continuing and baleful influence of Schleiermacher and his successors on the whole treatment of historical material. The result has often been steadfast refusal to take seriously the findings

of archeological and linguistic research. We believe that there is less and less excuse for the resulting confusion in this latter half of the twentieth century. Closely allied with these presuppositions is the ever-present fog of existentialism, casting ghostly shadows over an already confused landscape. Existentialism as a method of interpreting the New Testament is based upon a whole series of undemonstrable postulates of Platonic, Neo-Platonic, left-wing scholastic, and relativistic origins. So anti-historical is this approach that it fascinates speculative minds which prefer cliches to factual data, and shifting ideology to empirical research and logical demonstrations.[3]

Why Is Some of the Bible Offensive?

Apart from questions of mythology, contradiction, conflict with science, and historical inaccuracy, people have rejected the Bible because the content of it is considered offensive. In particular, biblical expressions of the wrath of God have been singled out for criticism. The Old Testament is criticized for portraying a God who is merciless and arbitrary in His judgment. It is frequently stated, "I have no problems with the loving God of the New Testament, it is the angry God of the Old Testament I reject."

In such reactions to the Old Testament, we find serious misunderstandings of the wrath of God. Nowhere do we find God involved in capricious or arbitrary acts of judgment. His wrath is never directed against the innocent. His anger never flows without a reason. It is always directed against human rebellion and sin.

It is ironic that the two Testaments are so often placed in contrast to each other. The irony may be seen in light of the cross. It is the cross of the New Testament that reveals the most violent and mysterious outpouring of the wrath of God that we find anywhere in Scripture. Here an innocent man does suffer but only after He willingly takes upon Himself, by imputation, the sins of the world. Without this act of wrath there is no grace. But it is precisely through this act of wrath that grace is made available. The New Testament knows no disjunction between the God of Jesus and the God of Abraham. Jesus appeals to the God of the Old Testament fathers as the God He is serving and revealing.

The Old Testament, in spite of its manifestations of the wrath of God, remains a history of God's grace and long-suffering with a rebellious people. There is wrath unparalleled in the New Testament and grace overwhelming in the Old Testament. A false dichotomy between the Testaments is foreign to the biblical writers themselves.

When we examine the law code of Israel, however, do we not see a legal ethic that is in fact bloodthirsty? Does not the list of over 35 crimes which require capital punishment reflect a barbarian ethic? Are not the punitive measures of the Old Testament manifestations of what we would regard as cruel and unusual punishment?

The law code of the Old Testament seems harsh to us in light of our present societal standards. But we live in an age where serious sin is not taken seriously. We live in an age where the holiness of God and the sanctity of human life have been sadly eclipsed. If we compare the law of the Old Testament with the law of creation, we see not the cruelty of God but the mercy of God. In creation all sin against God is regarded as a capital offense. In the slightest act of rebellion we commit cosmic treason. Any sin against a perfectly holy and righteous God may justly culminate in death. Thus the Old

Testament law represents a massive *reduction* of capital crimes which reveals not the bloodthirsty vengeance of an angry God, but the long-suffering mercy of a holy and loving God.

It is precisely at the point of offense in Scripture that we meet a special opportunity for supernatural instruction. By studying the parts of Scripture that are offensive to us we have the opportunity to discover those values and concepts we hold that are out of harmony with the wisdom of God. If we are offended by the Bible, perhaps the fault is not in God but in our own corrupt and distorted sense of values. I wonder what would happen if we called a moratorium on our criticism of the Bible and allowed the Bible to criticize us!

Are Scriptures Infallible?

It is one thing to argue that the Bible is a basically reliable source of history and religious instruction; it is quite another thing to assert that the Bible is inspired, inerrant, and infallible. It is one thing to maintain that the Bible has great value as a treasury of human insight into religious truth; it is quite another to maintain that it provides us with divine revelation and can justly be called the Word of God.

Why do Christians go beyond asserting general reliability of the Bible to the conviction that the Bible is the infallible Word of God? What follows is not an attempt to present an argument for the infallibility of Scripture, but rather an attempt to outline the *procedure* by which such a conclusion is reached. It is beyond the scope of this work to provide a defense of biblical infallibility. Rather the aim is to explain and clarify the *process* by which the conclusion is reached.

The case for the infallibility of Scripture proceeds along both deductive and inductive lines. It moves from the premise of general trustworthiness to the conclusion of infallibility. The reasoning proceeds as follows:

Premise A—The Bible is a basically reliable and trust-worthy document.

Premise B—On the basis of this reliable document we have sufficient evidence to believe confidently that Jesus Christ is the Son of God.

Premise C—Jesus Christ being the Son of God is an infallible authority.

Premise D—Jesus Christ teaches that the Bible is more than generally trustworthy; it is the very Word of God.

Premise E—The word, in that it comes from God, is utterly trustworthy because God is utterly trustworthy.

Conclusion—On the basis of the infallible authority of Jesus Christ, the church believes the Bible to be utterly trustworthy, i.e., infallible.

Note that this progression does not involve *circular* reasoning. Circular reasoning occurs when the conclusion is already present in the first premise. Rather this method follows a *linear* pattern of development. The argument itself is not infallible as each premise involves matters of inductive or deductive reasoning that is done by fallible human beings. But there is no subjective leap of faith found in the method. Rather the process involves careful historical, empirical investigation as well as logical inferences.

That the Bible claims to be the Word of God is not enough to authenticate the claim. Any book can make such a claim. But the fact that the claim is made is significant indeed. If the Bible is trustworthy then we must take seriously the claim that it is more than trust-

31

worthy. If we are persuaded that Christ is the sinless Son of God then we must take seriously His view of Holy Scripture. If the church submits to the authority of Christ then it must regard His view of Scripture as being authoritative. It is from the impetus of Christ Himself that the church is led to confess her faith in the divine authority and infallibility of Holy Scripture.

In a symposium of biblical scholars and theologians that was held in the Ligonier Valley in Pennsylvania in the fall of 1973, a joint team of scholars issued a statement on Scripture that focuses on the authority of Christ as the ground-basis for biblical authority. This "Ligonier Statement" says:

> We believe the Holy Scriptures of the Old and New Testaments to be the inspired and inerrant Word of God: We hold the Bible, as originally given through human agents of revelation, to be infallible and see this as a crucial article of faith with implications for the entire life and practice of all Christian people. With the great fathers of Christian history we declare our confidence in the total trustworthiness of Scriptures, urging that any view which imputes to them a lesser degree of inerrancy than total, is in conflict with the Bible's self-testimony in general and with the teaching of Jesus Christ in particular. Out of obedience to the Lord of the Church we submit ourselves unreservedly to his authoritative view of Holy Writ.

Key Points to Remember

Why should you trust the Bible?

You should trust the Bible because the Bible has been proven trustworthy.

1. *The Bible does not have a mythical literary style as compared with other ancient literature.* The frequent charge that the Bible is "full of myths" is not warranted by facts. People should be encouraged to read the biblical accounts of miracles, the flood, and other controversial areas and compare them with other ancient sources that *do* use mythology as a literary style.

2. *Jewish-Christian history differs from the Greek view.* This significant difference is a crucial one to understand before we evaluate the historical credibility of the Bible.

3. *The Bible is not a science text but describes the world as it appears to the naked eye.* Biblical "conflicts" with science must be understood in terms of common-sense approaches to the "phenomenal" world. The concept of *phenomenological* description is important to master to be able to deal with this question. We should learn from the church's mistakes in the past—such as the case of Galileo.

4. *Variant accounts are not the same as contradictory accounts.* The charge that the Bible is "full of contradictions" is unwarranted. An understanding of the Law of Contradiction is vital to this question. Close scrutiny of biblical texts will show a difference between variant accounts and contradictory accounts.

5. *Modern historical research adds to biblical credibility.* Historical research and archeology have done much to vindicate the historical reliability and accuracy of the Bible. Important discoveries at Qumran, Ebla, Amarna and elsewhere have exploded the "assured results" of negative nineteenth-century criticism.

6. *The church's faith in the infallibility of Scripture is established on the basis of Christ's view of Scripture.* It involves a reasoning process which is *linear*, not circular. It moves from general reliability to a knowledge of

Christ to an acceptance of Christ's "infallible" view of Scripture.

Notes

1. A short bibliography of selected readings on this subject is included at the end of this book.
2. The Babylonian account of the Flood that covered the earth.
3. W.F. Albright and C.S. Mann, *Matthew*, Anchor Bible Series (New York: Doubleday, 1971), vol. 26, pp. 5,6.

two

"All Religions Are Good. It Doesn't Matter What You Believe."

America is a melting pot. People from every conceivable ethnic and religious background come together to form one nation—*e pluribus unum*, from the many, one. At the heart of our national sense of unity stands the crucial principle of religious toleration. Under the principle of religious toleration, all religious systems are guaranteed freedom of expression and equal treatment under the law. No one religion has exclusive claim to legal rights and government establishment. The government of the United States of America expresses the will of the founding fathers that there be no "established national religion." Thus, we have no state church that enjoys exclusive privilege under the law.

With the principle of equal toleration has come the idea that no religion has exclusive claims to truth.

Though the concept of legal religious toleration says nothing at all about the validity of true claims, many have drawn the implication that equal toleration means equal validity. Thus, when Christians or advocates of any religion make claims of exclusivity, their claims are often met with shock or anger at such a narrow-minded posture. To make exclusive religious claims is to fly in the face of national sentiment. It is like attacking baseball, hot dogs, motherhood, and apple pie (not to mention Chevrolet).

In the sixties the uplifted index finger became a symbol not only of a number one ranking for a favorite football team, but also a popular sign of the members of the "Jesus movement" that there is but "one way" to God, the way of Christ. The zeal of the Jesus People met great resistance and hostility at this point.

One of the most embarrassing moments I ever experienced came in a freshman English class in college. It was a time of painful public humiliation. The professor was a former war correspondent who was outwardly hostile to Christianity. In the middle of a class she looked at me and said, "Mr. Sproul, do you believe that Jesus Christ is the only way to God?" I gasped as I felt the weight of her question and knew that every eye in the room was on me. My mind raced for a way to escape my dilemma. I knew that if I said yes people would be angry. At the same time, I knew that if I said no I would be betraying Christ. Finally, I mumbled almost inaudibly, "Yes, I do." The teacher responded with unmitigated fury. She said in front of the whole class, "That's the most narrow-minded, bigoted, and arrogant statement I have ever heard. You must be a supreme egotist to believe that your way of religion is the only way." I made no reply but slouched rather meekly in my chair.

After the class was dismissed, I went to speak with my

teacher privately. In the conversation I tried to explain to her why I believed that Christ was the only way. I asked her if she thought that it was at least theoretically possible that Christ be one way to God. She allowed the possibility. I asked if she thought it were possible that without being narrow-minded or bigoted a person could come to the belief that Jesus was God. Though she did not believe in the deity of Christ, she recognized that people could, in fact, believe that without being bigoted. Then I explained to her that the reason I believed that Christ was the only way to God is because Christ Himself taught that. I reminded her that Jesus said, "I am the way, and the truth, and the life; no one comes to the Father, but by me" (John 14:6). I also pointed out that the New Testament refers to Christ as the "only-begotten" of the Father, and that "there is no other name under heaven through which men must be saved" (see Acts 4:12). I said to her, "Can you see that I am torn between loyalty to Christ and the modern spirit of pluralism?" I said, "Do you see that it is possible for me to believe in the uniqueness of Christ because He taught it? If I believed that Christ was the only way because I believe that my way must be the only way because it is my way, that would be an act of arrogance and egotism." She finally acknowledged that it was possible for someone to believe in the uniqueness of Christ without being arrogant and apologized sincerely to me. However, she went on to raise a more serious question than the question of my arrogance. She said, "How can you believe in a God who only allows one way to Himself? Isn't it narrow-minded of God to restrict redemption to one Saviour and one faith?"

Aren't All Religions Basically the Same?

In the final analysis this is the issue that must be

faced: Is God so narrow-minded that He provides only one way of redemption?

Part of the reason we struggle so deeply with a question like this is due to the impact of the results of the nineteenth-century approach to the study of comparative religion. In the nineteenth century there was a concerted effort by scholars to examine closely the distinctive characteristics of the major religions of the world. The "buzz word" of the day was "essence." Many serious studies of religion were published which contained titles like *The Essence of Religion* or *The Essence of Christianity*. These books reflected an attempt to get at the basic core of religious truth that was found in all religion.

Religion was often reduced to its lowest common denominator. Frequently the distilled essence of religion was pinpointed by the phrase "the universal fatherhood of God and the universal brotherhood of man." Thus it was seen that at the heart, all religions were working for the same thing. The outward trappings of religious belief and practice differed from culture to culture but at the root their goals were the same. Thus, if all religions were essentially the same then no one of them could ever make exclusive claims to validity.

Out of this quest for the essence of religion came the now famous and popular "mountain analogy." The mountain analogy pictures God at the peak of the mountain with man down at the base. The story of religion is the account of man's effort to move from the base of the mountain to the peak of fellowship and communion with God. The mountain has many roads. Some of the roads go up the mountain by a very direct route. Other roads wind in circuitous fashion all over the mountain, but eventually reach the top. Thus, according to the proponents of this analogy, all religious roads, though they differ in route, ultimately arrive at the same place.

Out of this conviction that all roads lead to God has come a considerable number of ecumenical movements, pan-religious endeavors, and even new religions such as Bahái which seek a total synthesis and amalgamation of all of the world religions into one new unified religion.

I once had a conversation with a Bahái priest. He told me that all religions were equally valid. I began to interrogate him concerning the points of conflict that exist between Islam and Buddhism, between Confucianism and Judaism, and between Christianity and Taoism. The man responded by saying that he didn't know anything about Islam, Judaism, or the rest but that he did know they were all the same. I wondered aloud how anyone could assert that all religions were the same when he had no knowledge of what those religions professed or denied. How can Buddhism be true when it *denies* the existence of a personal God and at the same time Christianity be true when it *affirms* the existence of a personal God? Can there be a personal God and not be a personal God at the same time and in the same relationship? Can Orthodox Judaism be right when it denies life after death and Christianity be equally right when it affirms life after death? Can classical Islam have a valid ethic that endorses the killing of infidels while at the same time the Christian ethic of loving your enemies be equally valid?

There are only two possible ways to maintain the equal validity of all religions. One is by ignoring the clear contradictions between them by a flight into irrationality; the other is by assigning these contradictions to the level of insignificant nonessentials. The latter approach involves us in a systematic process of reductionism. Reductionism strips each religion of elements considered vital by the adherents of the religion them-

39

selves and reduces the religion to its lowest common denominator. The distinctives of each religion are obscured and watered down to accommodate religious peace.

Why does this kind of reductionism take place? Perhaps there are many motivating factors for it. Certainly one of the most powerful factors is the desire to end religious controversies and the upheaval they often bring. Differences in religious conviction have led again and again to passionate disputes between people, family alienation, violent forms of religious persecution, and in many cases even war. Thus if we were able to achieve a universal religious essence perhaps we can end these very costly disputes. The goal is peace. The price is truth.

If religion deals with matters of ultimate concern, there is little wonder that religious debates produce so much passion. But if we are interested in truth we can never discover it by denying real differences of truth-claims. The peace that is produced by reductionism is a false and carnal peace. We recall the false prophets of Israel who, in their desperate attempts to avoid conflict, cried "Peace, peace," when there was no peace. Jeremiah's lament remains relevant, "These men heal the wounds of the daughters of Zion, slightly" (see Jer. 8:11).

It is one thing to seek an atmosphere of religious debate that is characterized by charity. It is quite another thing to say the matters under debate are not important. It is one thing to protect the right of every religious person to follow the dictates of his conscience without fear of persecution; it is another to say that opposing convictions are both true. We must note the difference between equal toleration under the law and equal validity according to truth.

40

Why Is God So Narrow-Minded?

We are still left with the problem, however, of a narrow-minded God who provides only one way of redemption. Does this not mean that people who live in a culture where that one religion is proclaimed have a decisive advantage over people living in other cultures? (The wider implications of this question are so important that I have devoted a separate chapter to the question of people who have never heard of Jesus Christ.) But let's examine the deeper question of the narrow-mindedness of God who provides only one way of redemption. We remember the words of Jesus when He said, "Broad is the way and wide is the gate that leads to destruction and many are they who go in thereby. But straight is the way and narrow is the gate that leads to life and few are those who find it" (see Matt. 7:13). What kind of a God would have such a narrow gate? The question implies a serious accusation; that God has not done enough to provide redemption for mankind.

Let us examine the accusation from a hypothetical perspective. Let us suppose that there is a God who is altogether holy and righteous. Suppose that God freely creates mankind and gives to mankind the gift of life. Suppose He sets His creatures in an ideal setting and gives them the freedom to participate in all of the glories of the created order with freedom. Suppose, however, that God imposes one small restriction upon them, warning them that if they violate that restriction, they will die. Would such a God have the right to impose such a restriction with the penalty of forfeiture of the gift of life if His authority is violated?

Suppose that for no just cause the ungrateful creatures disobeyed the restriction the moment God's back was turned. Suppose when He discovered their violation instead of killing them, He redeemed them. Suppose the

41

descendants of the first transgressors broadly and widely increased their disobedience and hostility toward their creator to the point that the whole world became rebellious to God, and each person in it "did what was right in his own eyes" (Judg. 21:25). Suppose God still determined to redeem these people and freely gave special gifts to one nation of people in order that, through them, the whole world would be blessed. Suppose God delivered this people from poverty and enslavement to a ruthless Egyptian Pharaoh. Suppose this privileged nation, as soon as it was liberated, rose up in further rebellion against their God and their liberator. Suppose they took His law and violated it consistently.

Suppose that God, still intent upon redemption, sent specially endowed messengers or prophets to plead with His people to return to Him. Suppose the people killed the divine messengers and mocked their message. Suppose the people then began to worship idols of stone and things fashioned by their own hands. Suppose these people invented religions that were contrary to the truth of the real God and worshiped creatures rather than the Creator.

Suppose in an ultimate act of redemption God Himself became incarnate in the person of His Son. Suppose this Son came into the world not to condemn the world, but to redeem the world. But suppose this Son of God were rejected, slandered, mocked, tortured, and murdered. Yet, suppose that God accepted the murder of His own Son as punishment for the sins of the very persons who murdered Him. Suppose this God offered to His Son's murderers total amnesty, complete forgiveness, transcendent peace that comes with the cleansing of all guilt, victory over death and an eternal life of complete felicity.

Suppose God gave these people as a free gift the

promise of a future life that would be without pain, without sickness, without death, and without tears. Suppose that God said to these people, "There is one thing that I demand. I demand that you honor my only-begotten Son and that you worship and serve Him alone." Suppose God did all of that, would you be willing to say to Him, "God, that's not fair, you haven't done enough"?

If man has in fact committed cosmic treason against God, what reason could we possibly have that God should provide any way of redemption? In light of the universal rebellion against God, the issue is not why is there only one way, but *why is there any way at all?* I know of no way of answering that question.

Why Do Christians Say that Christ Is God Incarnate?

At the heart of Christianity stands the person and work of Jesus Christ. His person and His work are part of the essence of Christianity. It is in who He is and what He has done that the essence of Christianity can be discovered. Both in His person and in His work we find elements of utter uniqueness. The Christian claim is that in the person of Jesus of Nazareth we meet God incarnate. Buddha never claimed to be anything more than a man. Mohammed claimed nothing more than to be a prophet. Moses and Confucius were mortals. If Christ was in fact God incarnate, then it is a travesty of justice to ascribe equal honor to Him and to the others. To do so would necessitate either falsely attributing to mortal man the attributes of deity or stripping Christ of His divine nature.

In the truth-claims of Christianity we find the notion of the sinlessness of Christ. If Jesus was in fact without sin, this would put Him in a class by Himself. If He had no other uniqueness, this one factor would set Him apart from every religious leader the world has ever known. Though claiming something does not make it true, nevertheless the fact that Jesus claimed to be sinless is significant. By that claim the religious stakes are established. If the claim is true, then Jesus' uniqueness is assured. If the claim is not true then Jesus fails to qualify as even one of many great religious teachers. He would only qualify as a hypocrite and a charlatan.

The claim of resurrection is vital to Christianity. If Christ has been raised from the dead by God, then He has the credential and certification that no other religious leader possesses. Buddha is dead. Mohammed is dead. Moses is dead. Confucius is dead. But, according to the truth-claim of Christianity, Christ is alive. If Christ has been vindicated by resurrection, His uniqueness as an object of religious devotion is established.

Another dimension of the uniqueness of Christ that is vital to Christianity is His work of atonement. Moses could mediate on the law; Mohammed could brandish a sword; Buddha could give personal counsel; Confucius could offer wise sayings; but none of these men was qualified to offer an atonement for the sins of the world.

It is not only the resurrection of Christ that makes Him unique but it is His death that puts Him in a class by Himself. His death was made as a payment for the sins of mankind. His sacrifice was perfect. Here we see the direct correlation between the uniqueness of His person, of His sinlessness, of His atoning death, and of His resurrection. Together these factors describe the only-begotten of the Father.

It is a mistake, indeed a fatal mistake, to assume that God is pleased by "religion." The cliche that "it doesn't matter what you believe as long as you are sincere" involves a devastating error. We can be sincerely wrong and miss the way of redemption offered by God. What we believe in and who we believe in makes an ultimate difference to our destiny. "Religion" can be a substitute for truth; a man-made system of distorting the revelation of God.

Christ alone is worthy of unlimited devotion and service. His total value sets Him apart from all pretenders to the throne. He alone is able to redeem. He alone is worthy of worship.

The exclusiveness of the Christian truth-claim must always rest on the uniqueness of Christ. Christians are not immune from arrogance and bigotry. Yet arrogance and bigotry have no ally in Christ. Christ's critique of these evil practices is more severe than any critic of Christianity can muster. At the same time this one who is so critical of arrogance and bigotry calls us to a single-minded devotion to truth. He claims to be that truth.

Key Points to Remember
Are all religions good? Does it matter what you believe?

1. *Religious toleration does not mean equal validity of truth.* The problem of exclusive claims to truth is deeply rooted in our culture. We must keep in mind the difference between *religious toleration* as a matter of legal rights and the concept of the *equal validity* of truth-claims.

2. *Objective evidence, not arrogance, must be the basis for Christian truth-claims.* Christians must guard against communicating a sense of arrogance about their convictions. The uniqueness of Christ must be established on the basis of *objective evidence* rather than by personal preference.

3. *All religions do not teach the same thing but differ at key points.* Attempts to make all religions "basically the same" involves the serious problem of reductionism

45

—reducing everything to a broad common denominator. Analogies such as the "mountain analogy" obscure the real and crucial differences between world religions.

4. *The uniqueness of Christ and His own exclusive claims are the heart of the issue.* To understand that uniqueness we must understand the whole pattern of biblical history. If the biblical history is true, then we can never suppose that God "has not done enough" to provide for our redemption.

5. *In light of biblical history it is easy to see why there is only "one way."*

6. *In spite of the fact that the world has been in constant rebellion to Him, God has provided a way of redemption.* The ultimate question of redemption is the question why God would bother to provide *any* way of redemption for us. The wonderful truth is that even though we don't deserve it, in Christ "we have redemption through his blood, . . . according to the riches of his grace" (Eph. 1:7).

three

"What About the
Poor Native Who Never
Heard of Christ?"

As a teacher of theology I am regularly faced with a plethora of questions raised by inquiring students. Though I've never tabulated these queries with a computer, I am convinced there is one question that heads the list in terms of numerical frequency. The question most often raised is, "What happens to the poor innocent native in Africa who has never heard of Christ?" The query expresses a deep concern for the person who dwells in remote parts of the earth, far removed from the exposure of modern media of communication. This person lives and dies without hearing a single word of the biblical message. Where does that person stand with God?

Why is this question asked so frequently? Why are so many students plagued by it? Perhaps there are several factors that stimulate the inquiry. First of all, people in the Western world are acquainted enough with Christianity to have some idea of the central motif of the love of God. Add to that the common understanding that at the core of the Christian faith is the assertion of the unique importance of the person and work of Christ. If Christ is unique and is necessary for redemption, how can one avail himself of this redemption if he has no knowledge of it? If God is so loving, why does He not light up the skies with a celestial message that is broadcast so clearly that none could possibly miss it? Why is the "good news" of redemption in Christ limited to those living in cultures that have access to it?

The question is stimulated not only by matters of speculative theology but also by a spirit of human compassion. If compassion resides within us at all, we must be ever sensitive to those who live in less privileged circumstances than we. We are not concerned here with a paternalistic or imperialistic sense of cultural privilege but with an ultimate sense of redemptive privilege. There can be found no intrinsic sense of righteousness within us that would induce God to make the means of redemption available to us in a privileged way. It might even be argued that our "privilege" is rooted in our greater need for redemption owing to our greater corruption. However, since sin is universal and not restricted to either civilized or uncivilized, Western or non-Western humanity, we can hardly find the answer there.

What Happens to the Innocent Person Who Never Heard of Christ?

Regardless of the motivations for it, we are still faced with the question. What does happen to the innocent person who has never heard of Christ?

The way the question is phrased will affect the answer given. When we ask, "What happens to the *innocent* person who has never heard?" we are loading the question with significant assumptions. If the question, however, is asked in this manner the answer is easy and is obvious. The innocent native who never hears of Christ is in excellent shape, and we need not be anxious about his redemption. The *innocent* person doesn't need to hear of Christ. He has no need of redemption. God never punishes innocent people. The innocent person needs no Saviour; he can save himself by his innocence.

When the question is framed in this way, however, it betrays the assumption that there are innocent people in this world. If that is so (an assumption which Christianity emphatically denies), then we need not be concerned about them. But we are faced still with the larger question, "What happens to the *guilty* person who has never heard?"

The assumption of innocence often slips into the question unnoticed. What is often meant is not a perfect innocence, but a relative innocence. We observe that some persons are more wicked than others. The wickedness appears all the more wicked when it occurs within a context of privilege. When a person lives wickedly knowing the details of God's commandments and has been instructed in them repeatedly, his wickedness appears heinous when measured against those who live in relative ignorance.

On the other hand, if the remote native is guilty, wherein lies his guilt? Is he punished for not believing in a Christ of whom he never heard? If God is just, that cannot be the case. If God were to punish a person for not responding to a message he had no possibility of hearing, that would be a gross injustice; it would be radically inconsistent with God's own revealed justice.

We can rest assured that no one is ever punished for rejecting Christ if they've never heard of Him.

Before we sigh too deep a breath of relief, let us keep in mind that the native is still not off the hook. Some have stopped at this point in their consideration of the question and allowed their sigh of relief to lull them too quickly into a comfortable ease about the question. The unspoken assumption at this point is that the only damnable offense against God is rejection of Christ. Since the native is not guilty of this we ought to let him alone. In fact letting him alone would be the most helpful and redemptive thing we could do for him. If we go to the native and inform him of Christ, we place his soul in eternal jeopardy. For now he knows of Christ, and if he refuses to respond to Him, he can no longer claim ignorance as an excuse. Hence, the best service we can render is silence.

But what if the above assumption is incorrect? What if there are other damnable offenses against God? That would change the situation and rouse us from our dogmatic slumbers. What if the person who has never heard of Christ has heard of God the Father and has rejected Him? Is rejection of God the Father as serious as rejection of God the Son? It would seem to be at least *as* serious if not more serious.

What About the Person Who Knows About God?

It is precisely at this point that the New Testament locates the universal guilt of man. The New Testament announces the coming of Christ to a world that had already rejected God the Father. Christ Himself said, "I came not to call the righteous, but the sinner to repentance. Those who are well have no need of a physician" (see Matt. 9:12,13).

The biblical response to the question of the person

50

who never heard of Christ is found in Romans 1, beginning with verse 18. The section begins with an awesome announcement of the revelation of the wrath of God:

> For the wrath of God is revealed from heaven against all ungodliness and wickedness of men who by their wickedness suppress the truth.

Notice that God's wrath is revealed not against innocence or ignorance but against ungodliness and wickedness. What kind of wickedness? Both the word "ungodliness" and the word "wickedness" are generic terms describing general classes of activity. What is the specific act that is provoking the divine wrath? The answer is clear, the *suppressing of truth.* We must ask, "What truth is being suppressed?" The rest of the text provides the answer:

> For what can be known about God is plain to them, because God has shown it to them. Ever since the creation of the world his invisible nature, namely, his eternal power and deity, has been clearly perceived in the things that have been made. So they are without excuse; for although they knew God they did not honor him as God or give thanks to him, but they became futile in their thinking and their senseless minds were darkened (Rom. 1:19-21).

Here the apostle gives us a description of what theologians call "general revelation." This means simply that God has revealed something generally. The "general" character of the revelation refers to two things, content and audience. The content is general in that it does not provide a detailed description of God. The trinity is not a part of this revelation. God reveals that He is, that He has eternal power and deity. The audience is general in that all men receive this revelation. God does not reveal Himself only to a small elite group of scholars or priests but to all mankind.

What else does this text teach about general revelation? First, we learn that it is clear and unambiguous. This knowledge is said to be *plain* (manifest) to them; that God has *shown* it to them; that it has been *clearly perceived*. Thus, this knowledge is not obscure.

Secondly, we learn that the knowledge "gets through" and finds its mark. God does not merely provide an available objective revelation of Himself that may or may not be subjectively received. We read, "They *knew* God." Man's problem is not that he doesn't know God but that he refuses to acknowledge what he knows to be true.

Thirdly, we learn that this revelation has been going on since the foundation of the world. It is not a once-for-all event but continues in a constant way.

Fourthly, we learn that the revelation comes by way of creation. God's invisible nature is revealed "through the things that are made." The whole creation is a glorious theater which gives a magnificent display of its creation.

Fifthly, we learn that the revelation is sufficient to render man inexcusable. The passage says, "So they are without excuse." What excuse do you suppose the apostle had in mind? What excuse does general revelation eliminate? Obviously the excuse eliminated is that of ignorance. If the apostle is correct about general revelation then none will ever be able to say to God, "I'm sorry I didn't worship and serve you. I didn't know you existed. If only I had known I most certainly would have been your obedient servant. I wasn't a militant atheist; I was an agnostic. I didn't think there was sufficient evidence to affirm your existence." If God has in fact clearly revealed Himself to all men, no man can plead ignorance as an excuse for not worshiping Him.

Ignorance may function as an excuse for certain things under certain circumstances. The Roman Catholic Church, in developing their moral theology, adopted a distinction between vincible ignorance and invincible ignorance. Vincible ignorance is that ignorance which could and should be overcome. It does not excuse. Invincible ignorance is that ignorance which could not possibly be overcome. It does excuse.

Suppose a person from Texas drove his car to California and came to San Francisco. Upon entering the city limits of San Francisco the motorist promptly ran a red light. A police officer accosted him and gave him a ticket for going through a red light. The motorist protested saying, "I did not know it was against the law to go through a red light in California. I am from Texas." Would this appeal to ignorance excuse the man? Certainly not. If the Texan presumes to drive his car in California, he is responsible to know the traffic laws. The laws are readily available and are not concealed by being locked up in a secret vault. This man's ignorance would be vincible, leaving him without excuse.

Suppose, on the other hand, that the city council of San Francisco were desperate for accumulating money quickly. Hence they meet in a secret conclave and pass a local municipal ordinance that outlaws driving through green lights and stopping at red lights. They decide the penalty for violating the law is a $100 fine. The catch is they decide not to notify the press or make any mention of the new secret law. The plan is to have a policeman at every intersection arresting motorists who stop on red and go on green. Could the arrested motorists plead ignorance as an excuse? Yes, their ignorance would be invincible and should excuse them.

53

Thus, the person who has never heard of Christ can plead ignorance at that point but cannot plead ignorance with respect to God the Father.

But aren't the people who live in remote areas of the world religious? Doesn't their religious activity remove them from any danger of the wrath of God? Isn't it true that many anthropologists tell us that man is *homo religiosus*, that religion is universal? Such people may not be educated or sophisticated in their religious activity. Perhaps they worship totem poles, cows, or bee trees. But at least they are trying and doing the best they can. They surely don't know any better. If they are born and raised in a culture that worships cows, how can they be expected to do any differently?

It is precisely at this point that the notion of general revelation is devastating. If Paul is correct, the practice of religion does not excuse the pagan but in fact compounds his guilt. How can that be? Paul continues his treatment of general revelation by saying:

> Claiming to be wise, they became fools, and exchanged the glory of the immortal God for images resembling mortal man or birds or animals or reptiles. Therefore God gave them up ... because they exchanged the truth about God for a lie and worshiped and served the creature rather than the Creator, who is blessed forever (Rom. 1:22-25).

Here the apostle examines pagan religion. He views it as a distortion of the truth. An "exchange" takes place between the truth of God and the lie. God's glory is replaced by the substitution of the "glory" of the creature. Creature worship is religion, but it is the religion of idolatry. To be zealous in the worship of idols is to be zealous in the insulting of the glory and dignity of God. If God clearly reveals His glory and that glory is replaced by the worship of creatures, the ensuing religion is not pleasing, but displeasing to God.

Thus the fact that people are religious does not in itself mean that God is pleased with them. Idolatry represents the ultimate insult to God. To reduce God to the level of the creature is to strip God of His deity. This is particularly odious to God in light of the fact that all men have received enough revelation about Him to know that He is not a creature. Pagan religion is viewed then not as growing out of an honest attempt to search for God, but out of a fundamental rejection of God's self-revelation.

How Are the Pagans Judged?

The New Testament makes it clear that people will be judged according to the light that they have. All the elements of the Old Testament Law are not known by people living in remote parts of the world. But we read that they do have a law "written on their hearts" (Rom. 2:15). They are judged by the law they do not know and are found wanting. No one keeps the ethic he has even if he invents it himself.

I counseled once with a college student who was in my office as a "captive audience." He had come at his mother's insistence. His mother was a zealous Christian who continuously sought to persuade her son to become a Christian. The son was deeply alienated and resisted her persuasion. His rebellion was radical as he opted for a life-style that was on a collision course with his family values. As he spoke to me he argued that everyone had the right to develop his own ethic. He believed in a "do your own thing" morality. He complained that his mother had no right to "shove religion down my throat."

I asked him why he objected to his mother's tactics.

If his mother followed his ethic she would have every right to shove religion down his throat. His mother's "thing" was shoving religion down people's throats. I explained to him that his mother was not being consistent with her own Christian ethic because she was so insensitive to her son. Yet she was being consistent with her son's ethic. As we talked, he came to realize that what he really believed was that people could do their own thing as long as their own thing did not impinge on his thing. He wanted one ethic for himself but quite another for everybody else. It is when we complain about other people's behavior that we reveal what our deepest views of ethics are.

The pagan in Africa has an ethic. But even that ethic is violated. Thus, he remains exposed to the judgment of God. So often the primitive is idealized as being untainted by the corruption of civilization. Such idealized descriptions, however, do not fit the facts.

Thus if a person in a remote area has never heard of Christ, he will not be punished for that. What he will be punished for is the rejection of the Father of whom he has heard and for the disobedience to the law that is written in his heart. Again, we must remember that people are not rejected for what they haven't heard but for what they have heard.

If all men have heard of the Father but naturally reject Him, then it follows that all men need to know of the redemption offered in Christ. To have no knowledge of Christ is to be in jeopardy because of the prior rejection of the revelation of the Father. But to hear of Christ and reject Him is to be in a state of double jeopardy. Now not only has the Father been rejected but the Son as well. Thus every time the gospel is proclaimed it bears a two-edged sword. To those who believe, it is the savor of glory. To those who reject, it is death.

How Can the Native Hear?

If the person who has never heard of Christ is in serious jeopardy, how can his plight be alleviated? The answer comes in a simple statement made by the apostle Paul:

> But how are men to call upon him in whom they have not believed? And how are they to believe in him of whom they have never heard? And how are they to hear without a preacher? And how can men preach unless they are sent? As it is written, "How beautiful are the feet of those who preach good news!" (Rom. 10:14,15).

Here the apostle reiterates the need for the mission of the church. Mission (from the Latin "to send") begins with the love of God. It is because God so loved the world that He "sent" His Son into the world. The mission of Christ was in behalf of those who had rejected the Father. The rejected Father sent the Son and the Son sent His church. That is the basis for the world mission of the church. It is the mandate of Christ that those who have not heard do hear. They cannot hear without a preacher, and there cannot be a preacher without a "sending." The mandate of Christ is that the gospel be preached in every land and nation, to every tribe and tongue, to every living person. If this mandate were carried out by the church, the question of what happens to those who never heard would be a moot one.

The Christian must ask a second question after he has dealt with the question of those who have never heard. The Christian must ask, "What happens to me if I never do anything to promote the world mission of the church?" If the Christian takes this question seriously then his response must be equally serious. His concern for the remote native must begin with compassion, and it must also culminate in a response of compassion.

The question of the fate of the person who never hears of Christ is one that must be answered not only with words but by action as well. The action of mission must be prompted not by paternalism nor by imperialism but by obedience to the "sending" of Christ. All men need Christ, and it is the duty of the church to meet that need.

Key Points to Remember

What about pagans who never hear?

1. All men know God the Father (Rom. 1:18ff). The problem of the pagan who has never heard the gospel is the problem of our universal fallenness. We must emphasize that God has revealed Himself to all men. All men know there is a God. Thus, no one can plead ignorance as an excuse for denying God.

2. All men distort and reject true knowledge of God. Since all men know God and all distort or reject that knowledge, they are not innocent.

3. There are no innocent people in the world. People who die without hearing the gospel will be judged according to the knowledge they have. They will be judged guilty for rejecting God the Father. God never condemns innocent people.

4. God judges according to the knowledge people have. Idolatry as a "religion" does not please God but adds insult to injury to the glory of God (see Isa. 42:8). Idolatry does not represent man's search for God but rather man's flight from God.

5. The gospel is God's gift of redemption for the lost. God sends Christ to give people an opportunity for redemption from the guilt they already have. If men reject Christ they face the double judgment of rejecting both the Father and the Son (see Col. 1:13-17).

6. The pagan needs Christ to reconcile him to God the

Father. Christ Himself viewed the pagan as being in a "lost" condition.

7. Christ commands the Church to make sure everyone hears the gospel (see Mark 16:15).

8. Rejection of Christ brings a double judgment (see 2 Tim. 4:1).

9. "Religion" does not redeem people but may add to their guilt.

four

"Christianity Is a Crutch for Weak People."

"Religion is the opiate of the masses." This oft repeated quote from Karl Marx captures a common view of religion. Religion is seen as an attractive intoxicant for the depressed, the downhearted, and the weak. Overpowered by the harsh realities of life, people turn for comfort and emotional support to religion. Religion offers "balm in Gilead" for those who have been brutalized by life. A parallel expression we hear is, "I don't feel the *need* of religion," as if the truth or falsehood of Christianity depended upon one's feeling of need. At the root of this criticism is the assumption that religion is purely a subjective or emotional matter that involves personal preferences stemming from needs and weaknesses.

In the world of secular philosophy, committed atheists have asked the question, "If there is no God, why are so many people involved in religion?" The atheist seeks to understand where religion came from and why it continues to persist in an enlightened age if there is no objective and real foundation for its existence. The most common answer is that man invents God out of the pressures of human fears and weaknesses.

Was Religion Invented to Tame Natural Forces?

The father of modern psychoanalysis, Sigmund Freud, was very much interested in discovering the answer to the question of the origin of religion. He proposed a very interesting and credible theory on the motives behind the human invention of religion.

The threat of nature which holds many mysteries and displays awesome powers of destructive force is "tamed" by postulating a God who can help men in the struggles of life. Freud says:

> There are the elements, which seem to mock at all human control: the earth, which quakes and is torn apart and buries all human life and its works; water, which deluges and drowns everything in a turmoil; storms, which blow everything before them; there are diseases, which we have only recently recognized as attacks by other organisms; and finally there is the painful riddle of death, against which no medicine has yet been found, nor probably will be. With these forces nature rises up against us, majestic, cruel and inexorable; she brings to our mind once more our weakness and helplessness, which we thought to escape through the work of civilization.[1]

Given the threat of nature, Freud sees man going through a process of humanizing and personalizing nature. Religion begins by attributing human characteristics and personality to impersonal forces such as

61

earthquakes and storms. If a human being is angry with me and threatens to harm me, I can do several things to dissuade him. I can plead for mercy; I can flatter and praise him to try to get him to like me; I can offer to provide services for him if he treats me kindly; I can try to bribe him. There are a host of ways to deal with human anger. We understand personal anger bcause we deal with it every day. But how do you negotiate with a hurricane? You can't bribe it or plead with it to go away. It has no checking account and no ears to hear your pleas for mercy. Freud answers that man deals with the impersonal forces of nature by personalizing them via religion. You invent a spirit that lives in the storm or the flood. If the spirits are personal then all the forces of personal persuasion can be brought to bear on them. From a simple form of animistic spirit-powers inhabiting nature, man develops a more sophisticated religion of monotheism. In the monotheism all the pleading, bargaining, praise, and service can be focused on one personal deity who has control of all nature. The ultimate crutch then becomes a personal God, a combination of kindly grandfather, cosmic bellhop, and celestial bodyguard. By religion, nature is made sacred and personal so that its threatening power is brought under control.

Is Religion an Invention of the Rich?

Karl Marx explains the origin and function of religion in economic terms. It is not so much the hurricane that provokes religious interest as it is the cruel forces of economic conflict. Marx sees religion as the invention of the controlling economic classes. The ruling classes are in a minority, and they accumulate an inordinate amount of wealth. With wealth and luxury in the hands of a few, the rich, he says, are always afraid of an uprising by the poor masses. If the masses ever find out how much collective power they have and revolt against the rich, the rich are in trouble. So how does the minority control the majority? They invent a religion that does several things to protect their vested interests. The religion emphasizes such virtues as industry, service, humility, and obedience. This religious "ethic" helps keep the masses in line.

The religion also provides comfort and consolation to the weak and needy and gives a kind of "spiritual" dignity to the oppressed. The big prize that religion offers the workers is the promise of pie-in-the-sky in the next life. If the worker refrains from violent revolution and the love of money in this life, God will reward him with milk and honey and streets of gold in heaven. In the meantime, the rich enjoy their milk, honey, and gold right now. The ethic and the promise keep the masses intoxicated with a kind of opium. They are drugged by religion and kept in a kind of euphoric stupor while the rich continue to exploit them.

Other similar theories of the origin of religion have been set forth by Nietzsche, Feuerbach, Russell, Sartre, and others. Though the theories differ in points of detail, they contain a common element of argumentation. The idea that religion owes its origin and its sustaining power to psychological needs runs as a common thread through all of them.

A few important things must be said at the outset of any serious response to these theories and objections. There is no dispute that man has the power of creative imagination and the capacity to turn his fantasies into theories or full-blown religious systems. It must also be admitted that man does find in religion an important resource for comfort and consolation. That people are often attracted to religion by emotional needs is not in dispute. That religion has been used countless times in

63

history as a tool of exploitation is not in dispute. But the same thing can be said for atheism.

There are profound psychological reasons that motivate people toward the rejection of religion. Being mistreated by a priest, disillusioned by a "religious" parent (as Marx was), being exploited by a religious charlatan, can all be subjective motives for the rejection of faith. The atheist has his vested interests too. A man burdened by serious guilt may want very much for there to be no God. A man wanting to indulge his own desires at the expense of others may like the idea that he is not ultimately accountable to a just and holy God.

If There Is No God Why Is There Religion?

The theories of the origin of religion set forth by Freud and the others offer no proof or falsification of the case of theism. The nonexistence of God is assumed. Their question is, "If there is no God why is there religion?" If indeed there is no God then their theories of the origin of religion are plausible. But first it must be established that in fact there is no God. That man has the ability to invent religion is obvious. That he in fact did invent religion is not so obvious.

In a courtroom in criminal trial the question of means and motive are relevant. If the prosecutor can prove that the accused had the means to commit the crime and a strong motive for doing it, this helps his case. If the defense can prove that his client had neither means nor motive, it goes a long way to establish his innocence. But the prosecutor must prove more than the means and the motive of the defendant. He must show evidence that the accused actually did commit the crime. If a person is murdered, a large number of people could be found who had the means and motive to commit murder.

The question of the origin of religion (or the origin of

anything) is not fundamentally a psychological question but an historical one. Psychology plays a definite role but cannot be the decisive factor in determining what in fact did happen in the past. If the believer has only one argument for the existence of God—namely, that the existence of religion proves the existence of God—then the Freudian hypothesis would be devastating. Indeed it would be strange if there were a God and no one believed in Him, but the presence of believers or absence of believers could not determine the issue by itself. It is both theoretically possible that there be a God with no one believing in Him and that there is no God while everyone believes He exists. The truth of reality is not determined by counting noses.

Though the atheist offers an interesting study of psychological motives for religious belief, he must also recognize that the New Testament offers some interesting input about the psychological motives for atheism.

The apostle Paul offers a counteroffensive to the atheist in his Epistle to the Romans. He says:

> For the wrath of God is revealed from heaven against all ungodliness and wickedness of men who by their wickedness suppress the truth (Rom. 1:18).

Paul elaborates his theme of general revelation arguing that God has clearly revealed Himself to all men through the created order. He maintains that all men "clearly perceive" this revelation. However man "represses" or "suppresses" this knowledge. The word he uses is the Greek term *katakein*. This word has been translated variously by "stifle," "hold down," "suppress," "repress," and "hinder." J.H. Bavinck writes:

> It seems to me that in this case we should translate it by "repress." We intentionally choose a word which has a specific meaning

in psychological literature. Webster's *New Collegiate Dictionary* defines "repression" as the "process by which unacceptable desires or impulses are excluded from consciousness and thus being denied direct satisfaction are left to operate in the unconscious." This seems to agree with what Paul says here about human life. But we must mention that the word repression has received a wider meaning in more recent psychology. In Freudian psychology it specifically refers to unconscious desires of a more or less sexual nature. In more recent psychology it is also applied to desires or impulses of a very different nature. The impulses or desires which are repressed may be very valuable. Any thing that goes contrary to the accepted patterns of life or to the predominant popular ideas may be repressed. Usually this happens and results can be far-reaching. We are reminded of this psychological phenomenon recently discovered by Paul's use of the word. He says that man always naturally represses God's truth because it is contrary to his pattern of life.[2]

Thus Paul says that man receives a clear revelation from God but represses that truth and refuses to acknowledge what he knows to be true. He has a negative psychological reaction to the knowledge of God. There is a sense in which the knowledge of God is traumatic to people. It provokes fear and dread.

Paul goes on to say in the same context that man "exchanges the truth of God for a lie and serves the creature rather than the Creator" (see Rom. 1:23). This exchange or "substitution" of idolatry for authentic religion indicates that the repressed knowledge is not actually destroyed. In traumatic experiences the memory is not obliterated but forced down into the unconscious. The "knowledge" is not destroyed and will work its way back to the surface in veiled or disguised forms. Psychiatrists in treating patients pay close attention not only to the words that are spoken but to the nonverbal actions that accompany the words. When a patient has a noticeable "tic" every time his mother is mentioned, the doctor knows this is significant. Dream interpretation is another means of exploring veiled and disguised memory images.

Translating this to religious terms we see that man has a propensity to soften his understanding of God by creating images of God in religious garb that are non-threatening. It is common for people to speak of belief in "higher power" or as "something greater than ourselves." These faceless, nameless deities are abstractions which make no personal demands upon us. "Religion" may represent human attempts to tame God or remove the threat of His truth from us. It is one thing to believe in a "higher power"; it is another to believe in a holy personal God who makes ultimate demands upon us and before whom we are ultimately accountable. To postulate the belief in a nebulous "higher power" is to hedge a bit between atheism and a full-bodied Christianity with its personal demands.

Why Are We Afraid of God?

If Paul is correct and it is true that God has revealed Himself to all men, what is it about Him that would terrify us so much and lead us into this exchange-substitution process? There is much about God that can evoke negative feelings of terror. Perhaps the five most significant aspects of His being that make us uncomfortable are: 1) His holiness, 2) His omniscience, 3) His sovereignty, 4) His omnipotence, and 5) His immutability.

The threat of holiness. Rudolf Otto did a massive study of the effect on people of various cultures of the experience of the holy. He discovered that mankind from the Fiji Islands to Washington, D.C. have a strong sense of ambivalence to the holy. Mixed feelings of dread and fascination seem to accompany such experiences. The biblical record uniformly relates that when men confront the holy they are reduced to a state of terror.

The prophet Isaiah recorded his experience in the Temple of encountering a vision of the Holy God of Israel. The effect of the experience was a threat of disintegration.

> In the year that King Uzziah died I saw the Lord sitting upon a throne, high and lifted up; and his train filled the temple. Above him stood the seraphim; each had six wings: with two he covered his face, and with two he covered his feet, and with two he flew. And one called to another and said: "Holy, holy, holy is the LORD of hosts; the whole earth is full of his glory." And the foundations of the thresholds shook at the voice of him who called, and the house was filled with smoke. And I said: "Woe is me! For I am lost; for I am a man of unclean lips, and I dwell in the midst of a people of unclean lips; for my eyes have seen the King, the LORD of hosts!" (Isa. 6:1-5).

What does Isaiah mean when he says that he is "undone" *(KJV)* after beholding the vision of the holiness of God? If we translate this word into contemporary categories of speech we could describe it in terms of the psychological process of disintegration. Isaiah is "coming apart" or "breaking down." His self-image is shattered and his sense of wholeness or integration is annihilated. Why? Where formerly he judged himself by comparing himself to other fallen human beings and thus came to a high opinion of himself, he now measures himself against the ultimate standard of holiness. In the vision experience Isaiah not only finds out who God is, but he also finds out who Isaiah is. His self-image is shattered as he sees himself as a man of unclean lips. The same experience of personal disintegration is recorded by Job and by the prophet Habakkuk.

Another strange example of men's reaction to the holy may be seen in the biblical incident of Jesus' stilling the tempest:

> And leaving the crowd, they took him with them, just as he was, in the boat. And other boats were with him. And a great storm of wind arose, and the waves beat into the boat, so that the boat was already filling. But he was in the stern, asleep on the cushion; and they woke him and said to him, "Teacher, do you not care if we perish?" And he awoke and rebuked the wind, and said to the sea, "Peace! Be still!" And the wind ceased, and there was a great calm. He said to them, "Why are you afraid? Have you no faith?" And they were filled with awe, and said to one another, "Who then is this, that even the wind and the sea obey him?" (Mark 4:36-41).

Here we have a unique combination of a description of men's fear of the power of nature coupled with the human fear of the holy. Note that the narrative speaks of the fishermen's fear of the sudden tempest. Yet, after the tempest has ceased and the sea is calmed they become "very much afraid." When the threat of nature

69

is removed their fear is not eliminated but increased. Now they are more afraid of Jesus than they were of the storm. They say, "Who then is this?" Other translations read, "What manner of man is this?" There was no safe category in which they could put Jesus and disarm Him. He was in a class by Himself, a class that was utterly alien—the class of the Holy.

The same response is expressed by Peter after Jesus has his nets filled to the breaking point following a frustrating night of fishing without success. Instead of asking Jesus to go into the fishing business with him, Peter exclaims, "Depart from me, for I am a sinful man, O Lord" (Luke 5:8). Peter articulates a common human desire, that we be removed to a safe distance from the Holy.

At this point I must challenge Freud's thesis that the fear of nature is the chief factor in the origin of Christianity. To be sure the personal non-holy is less threatening than the impersonal non-holy. But what about the personal Holy? Man may indeed invent a personal deity to protect him from nature. But would he invent a personal Holy deity whose holiness is even more dreadful than the forces of nature?

The threat of omniscience. One of our greatest fears in this life is that our most closely-guarded secrets might be exposed. We like privacy and choose our intimate confidants very carefully. There are closely guarded skeletons in everybody's closet. The specter of an Orwellian "big brother" who observes our every move is most unpopular. Jean Paul Sartre has written extensively of the feeling of "shame-consciousness" that goes with the experience of being watched through a keyhole. The biblical imagery of "nakedness" calls attention to the same discomfort of shame. The first awareness of man after the Fall was expressed not in overt terms of guilt but in an awareness of nakedness. The first action of man after the Fall was to hide himself from the gaze of God.

If God is omniscient then every closet is transparent. There is nowhere to hide. He cannot be deceived or avoided; there can be no cover-up. Again and again the cry of the biblical character caught in the grips of personal guilt is that God should not look at him. When we commit acts of evil we do not want God to look at us but to overlook us. Kierkegaard said, "Man lives incognito throughout his life."

That man fears the gaze of an omniscient God is an important part of the background for the biblical notion of the cross. The New Testament frequently speaks of the righteousness of Christ serving as a "covering" for man. If we are uncomfortable in our moral nakedness, we can go to Christ for a cover or we can seek to deny that anybody is at the keyhole.

The threat of sovereignty. If anything about God provokes negative psychological reactions, it is His law. Over against all of our self-interests stands the absolute law of God. If there is a God, then I am not free to do as I please. I may have a measure of freedom, but I can never be autonomous. I can never have an absolute license to "do my own thing." But if there is no God then, as Dostoyevsky said, "All things are permissible." Thus God's sovereignty is on a collision course with my own evil desires. The primordial temptation offered by the serpent was, "You will not die, but you shall be as gods" (see Gen. 3:5). But if God is, I cannot ever be a god. The desire for absolute freedom is strong in the corrupt heart of man. To achieve such freedom God must be destroyed or denied. The nebulous "higher power" is a God without sovereignty, a God without a law.

The problem of guilt is one of the most paralyzing

71

factors in human life. Any psychiatrist knows how devastating guilt can be to the human personality. But when real guilt is acquired there are basically two things we can do about it. We can deny it, or we can seek to have it forgiven. The first alternative seems to be the least painful, but it doesn't work. The guilt is real and requires real forgiveness. At the heart of the attempt of man to deny the existence of guilt is the urgent need of man to be free of his guilt. If we get rid of God, we get rid of guilt.

The attempt to circumvent the sovereignty of God and be free of guilt takes subtle forms. Not everyone forcefully denies the existence of God. Rather God's nature is reshaped into a deity whose only attribute is love. God is stripped of His wrath, justice, and sovereignty; He is left clad only with a maudlin kind of love that makes no demands. This kind of God requires no repentance but exhibits a kind of love that means "never having to say that you are sorry." This stripped, weak, helpless God is the God of a very popular American religion. But it is not Christianity.

The threat of omnipotence. Power is one of the most intimidating devices that men exploit to gain their goals. The carrying of a "big stick" can provoke great fear. Policemen have nicknamed their nightsticks "persuaders." They know that instruments of force produce a certain psychological response. If we tremble at a nightstick which represents limited, finite power how much more intimidated are we by one who rules with absolute power. He is sometimes called a "higher" power, but why isn't He referred to as an "absolute power"? Even the term "higher power" represents an attempt to escape the absolute character of God's power.

This attribute of God is enough in itself to provoke a prejudicial vote for atheism. Perhaps we fear that God's absolute power will be wielded against us in a tyrannical way. We hear that power corrupts and that absolute power corrupts absolutely. In saying that we forget that with God absolute power is coupled with absolute holiness. (Maybe that is why we fear it so much.) When we add to that absolute power, absolute holiness, absolute omniscience, and absolute sovereignty, we are overwhelmed. In contrast to God I am impotent. Atheism, however, gives me the opportunity to "kick sand in the face of God."

The threat of immutability. Why would the unchanging character of God be an attribute that threatens us? This attribute cannot be viewed in isolation from the rest. In relationship to God's other attributes this one is the clincher. For with God's immutability all hope that God will ever change vanishes. There is no hope that tomorrow God will compromise His holiness. There is no chance that God will ever fall and become tainted with sin as we are. There is not the remotest possibility that God will be afflicted with hardening of the arteries and begin to have lapses of memory. His eyesight will never become dim so we can escape His gaze. His omnipotence will never be diminished by muscle atrophy and feebleness. His sovereignty will never be overthrown by a coup d'etat. Whatever God is now, He will be forever. Thus, if I am going to get along with God, it is I who must change, not He.

God reveals Himself to us as a formidable opponent. He evokes such feelings of dread within us that our reasoning about Him might easily be clouded. Religion, indeed, might be used as a crutch; but the atheist must also acknowledge that the crutch might be needed for the other foot.

It must be said that pointing out the possible reasons why prejudice can be a factor in religious conclusions is not enough to demonstrate the existence of God. Being aware of these potential and actual points of prejudice is important to the discussion on both sides. When we are dealing with the question of the existence of God, we are dealing with an issue in which we all have an ultimate vested interest. No one can deal with the question with a totally dispassionate attitude; there is too much at stake. There are times when we need to "train the guns" on ourselves to check our own vested interests. The most devout Christian may have already allowed his own prejudices to soften his view of God. Let us deal with the biblical God on the terms in which He is presented in the Bible. If we reshape Him and "create Him in our own image" then we will have obscured His real identity. The truth can never be determined by what we want it to be. God may, in fact, be everything we want Him to be, but if that is so, it is not because He shapes Himself according to our desires. If He is, He is what He is in and by Himself. If He is not, all my desires about Him are impotent and futile.

The question of Christianity and truth cannot be affirmed or denied simply by examining human need and prejudice. Prejudice works on both sides of the issue. If I feel the need of religion, that cannot validate its claims. If I do not feel the need of religion, that does not negate or falsify its claims.

Key Points to Remember
Is Christianity a crutch for weak people?

1. *We all need a crutch.* In a sense we must agree that Christianity is a crutch for weak people. But because we are all crippled, it is a crutch we all need. The question is, does the crutch have any basis in reality or is it an artificially devised aid? Do we "invent" God because we need Him?

2. Psychological needs may prompt us to invent God. We must admit to the Freuds and Sartres of this world that we do want there to be a God and that we would be capable of inventing "God" even if there was none. We must acknowledge that there are many things about life that threaten us, such as the force of nature, the danger of disease, and the inevitable threat of death.

3. Psychological needs may also prompt us to deny God. God is a threat to us too. Atheism may also be positioned as a crutch motivated by a desire to escape the judgment of God. The atheist must acknowledge that the crutch may be for the "other foot."

4. The biblical God is more threatening than nature itself.

5. God's holiness, omniscience, sovereignty, omnipotence, and immutability make Him an awesome threat to us (see Ps. 38:1-4).

6. Even Christians "water-down" the character of the biblical God. The Christian God is "awesome" and we frequently water-down His character within the Christian church.

7. The truth of Christianity cannot be determined by psychology. A study of human needs and prejudices teach us a lot about ourselves but nothing about whether or not God really exists. We must note the crucial difference between the question of how religion *could have* started and how it, in fact, *did* start.

Notes

1. Sigmund Freud, *The Future of an Illusion*, trans. by W.P. Robson-Scott (New York: Doubleday & Company, 1964), p. 20.
2. J.H.Bavinck, *The Church Between the Temple and Mosque* (Grand Rapids: Eerdmans, n.d.), pp. 118,119. Used by permission.

"The Church Is Full of Hypocrites."

For many, particularly the young, our times are seen as days of disillusionment. Confidence in public institutions has been eroded. Some express anger and bitterness, while others exhibit a spirit of mourning about the loss of integrity in American institutions. There is resentment toward government, hostility toward business corporations, indifference to educational institutions, and a general distrust of the "system." The organized church has not escaped this spirit of disillusionment. In some respects the church has been a focal point of criticism. People expect much from the church and when she disappoints them, the pain can be severe. It is often in the context of such disappointment that the complaint is uttered, "The church is full of hypocrites."

We live in a rapidly changing culture. A host of traditional values have been jettisoned as so much excess baggage. Yet one such value is still regarded with some importance, the value of honesty. The Watergate tragedy revealed many things about us. One revelation of the episode was that people still demand honesty in their government officials. Fraud, conspiracy, deceit, and cover-up remain "ugly" words in our vocabulary.

Though honesty is still cherished as a virtue, it is very painful and at times almost impossible for us to admit it when we compromise it. On the one hand honesty is seen as a redemptive virtue that "atones" for a multitude of sins. We hear, "I may drink too much, but at least I admit it," or "I may play around sexually, but I'm no hypocrite; I'm honest about it."

Yet we rarely hear, "I know I'm a liar, but at least I'm honest about it." It is hard for us to say, "I lied." It is easier to say, "I made a mistake." When we are dealing with the problem of hypocrisy we are dealing with the problem of the lie. Fraudulent behavior involving dishonesty and deception are the major ingredients of hypocrisy. The hypocrite is one engaged in intentional deception. He pretends to be more righteous than he actually is. The hypocrite is a moral playactor. He lives a lie. He claims to be free of faults which he practices covertly. His life is a guarded sham.

With such a definition of hypocrisy in view, is it proper to say the church is *full* of hypocrites? If the church is not guilty of such a serious charge then she is a victim of slander. If she is guilty of such a charge, her guilt would be weighty indeed.

If the church is not full of hypocrites, why would so many people make the charge? There are several reasons why many honestly believe the church is loaded to capacity with hypocrites. Let us examine a few of them.

Is the Church Full of Sinners?

Frequently the words "sinner" and "hypocrite" are confused. The confusion is one that is commonly found between genus and species. Sinner is the generic term. Hypocrite is the species. Since hypocrisy is a sin, we can say, "All hypocrites are sinners." But we must not view this statement as an equation of identity. We cannot reverse the statement and say, "All sinners are hypocrites." Let us use the standard syllogism to clarify the confusion:

> The church is full of sinners
> *hypocrites are sinners*
> ... the church is full of hypocrites.

What is wrong with the syllogism? Here we see one of the most common fallacies committed in logic; the fallacy of the undistributed middle term. A similar incorrect syllogism may illustrate the problem further:

> The church is full of sinners
> *murderers are sinners*
> ... the church is full of murderers.

What happens is that people observe church members sinning. They reason within themselves, "That person professes to be a Christian. *Christians aren't supposed to sin.* That person is sinning; therefore, he is a hypocrite." The unspoken assumption is that a Christian is one who claims he does not sin. In reality just the opposite is the case. For a Christian to be a Christian, he must first be a sinner. Being a sinner is a prerequisite for being a church member. The Christian church is one of the few organizations in the world that requires a public acknowledgment of sin as a condition for membership. In one sense the church has fewer hypocrites than any institution because by definition the church is a haven for sinners. If the church claimed to be an organization of perfect people then her claim would be hypocritical.

But no such claim is made by the church. There is no slander in the charge that the church is full of sinners. Such a statement would only compliment the church for fulfilling her divinely appointed task.

Is the Church Empty of Hypocrites?

A second reason why people are inclined to believe the church is full of hypocrites is because there are, in fact, hypocrites in the church. Christians are guilty of all sorts of sins, including the sin of hypocrisy. Though the church may not be full of hypocrites, it is by no means empty of them. Christians are not above pretending to be more righteous than they are. Nor is everyone in the church who professes to be a Christian a true believer. There are various forms of hypocrisy and most of them are manifested to some degree in the church.

Hypocrisy of faith. One form of hypocrisy found in the church is that which involves an insincere profession of faith. Some people join the church under false pretensions. In many communities it is still fashionable to belong to a church. Thus, people join for social status or because they have friends or family who are members. I've heard businessmen tell me they maintain church membership because it provides customer contacts and aids in business relationships and provides an aura of "respectability."

As Christ Himself predicted, the church always has an admixture of "tares and wheat" of true believers and false (see Matt. 13:24-30).

Some "unbelievers" are church members not because they willfully and deceitfully give a pretense of faith but because the church neither requires nor makes clear a decisive confession of faith. In their zeal to gain membership or be all-inclusive in spirit, some churches ignore their own standards for membership. In this case it is not the individual "unbeliever" who is being hypocritical but the church itself who misleads or misinforms the applicant for membership.

Hypocrisy in vows. If there is any area in the life of the church where the incidence of hypocrisy is at a very unhealthy rate, it is at the place of sacred vows. In most churches, membership is acquired only after a public profession of faith and stating of vows of obligation. These vows include such promises as to be (1) faithful in attendance of worship, (2) faithful in financial support of the church, (3) diligent in private and congregational use of the means of grace, and (4) submissive to the discipline of the officers of the church. Yet there are people who make such vows who are lax in church attendance, miserly in their giving, indifferent to the means of grace, and positively hostile to church discipline, arguing that their private morality is not the concern of the church.

The problem of membership vows came home to me when I encountered an irate man who was furious because his son had been dropped from the rolls of the church. He argued that the church was unloving for dropping his son and self-righteous for not considering him "good enough" to be a member. In his anger the man overlooked the fact that his son had made solemn vows five years earlier that he did not take seriously. He had not been inside the church for four years. He made no use of the means of grace nor did he support the church in his offerings. The church did not "drop" him suddenly but had made repeated overtures to him, and gently counseled and invited him to participate in the life of the church on several occasions. This man was utterly derelict in keeping his vows; yet when he was removed from membership, it was the church that was accused of hypocrisy. Had the man been as derelict in his commitment to a service club or a country club, he would have been expelled much sooner.

The marriage vows are also subject to hypocrisy. They are often taken with no regard to the sanctity and awesome responsibility of marriage. People stand before God, their family, friends, the church, and representatives of the state and publicly take oaths of permanent commitment. For some people the only time they come to the church is to seek a minister who will solemnize and bless their marriage. To take such vows with no serious intent of subsequent effort to honor them is an act of hypocrisy.

Are Ministers Hypocritical?

Clergymen are often singled out as being the most hypocritical of all people. "Practice what you preach," has become the axiomatic critique of the clergy. Ministers do not get an exemption from hypocrisy along with their certificate of ordination. Perhaps the clergy, more than any other group, are prone to this particular sin. In the first place, the clergy must live with high expectations from their congregations and with classical stereotypes molding their behavior. The temptation to fake a kind of piety that is not genuine is a great one.

There are many motives that lead men into the ministry. Some of these motives are noble; some are not so noble. A man may seek the ministry out of a profound faith and sincere desire to serve God. However, some are motivated by a strong sense of unbelief. How can that be? There are certain people who are so exercised about religion and theological questions that they find themselves in debates about religion every day. Many of these can be found on the college campuses. Their constant arguments about religion lead them to study it more and more, if for no other reason than to refute it.

Some of these people end up in seminary and carry their skeptical crusade throughout their entire lives from inside the church. It is a kind of "if you can't beat them, join them" syndrome.

Other motivations for ordination may include the desire to escape the draft (seminaries were unusually crowded during the Vietnam conflict); the desire to have a profession which gives opportunity for public leadership; family pressure ("my mother always wanted me to be a minister" syndrome); the desire to find a conduit for carrying out humanitarian programs; or even to silence the nagging guilt feelings that unbelief may bring.

On almost every occasion where Jesus is found rebuking hypocrisy in the New Testament, His words are directed against the clergy. It is the clergy He addresses in the most stinging terms saying: "Woe unto you scribes and Pharisees, hypocrites! You go over land and sea to make one convert and once you win him you make him twice the child of hell than you are yourselves" (see Matt. 23:15). Jesus spoke of the clergy of His day as being like whited mausoleums, painted white on the outside but inside filled with dead men's bones (see Matt. 23:27).

Are all ministers hypocrites? Certainly there is no minister in the world who practices perfectly what he preaches. If the pastor only could preach about what he himself has mastered, he would have precious little to preach about. That is one of the most difficult dimensions of being a minister. It is important to remember that the sermon is to be directed to the minister as well as the congregation. In fact, many such sermons are born out of the minister's own personal struggles. The minister is required to preach about the holiness of God and perfect obedience long before he himself is perfectly obedient. To preach at a higher level than you perform is not hypocrisy. To claim a higher level of performance than you have attained is hypocrisy.

Is Hypocrisy Serious?

Why does Christ take such a stern stance with respect to hypocrisy? In the record of His encounters with sinful people we find Him speaking with gentleness and tenderness. Yet, when He confronts the hypocrites, the tone of His remarks is severe. Maybe it has something to do with the enormous damage hypocrisy causes. When the fraud of the hypocrite is exposed, many people are hurt, disappointed, and disillusioned. One hypocrite can cause the loss not only of his own credibility but the credibility of his comrades and all they stand for. Jesus warned of leading the "little ones astray." Paul spoke of people blaspheming because of the bad conduct of the church.

We all know what it means to suffer the pain of disillusionment. The Watergate matter cannot be understood simply in terms of the nuances of politics. The President let the people down. He was not the first. I remember vividly the pain I felt when Ike denied Russian claims of our aerial spying in the fifties. I believed the President until the Russians produced the photograph of the captured Gary Powers. Eisenhower's lie was not the scandal of Watergate, but it began a series of problems that emerged in the so-called "credibility gap" between the American people and their government.

It is one thing to be disillusioned by your government, it is quite another to be disillusioned about God or about Christ. There are multitudes of people in the world who want nothing to do with Christ or His church because they have been violated by Christians. Gandhi rejected Christianity partly because he suffered at the hands of ruthless people calling themselves Christians. Countless people have been hurt and disappointed by ministers or priests. The effect can last for a long time.

To illustrate the long-range effects of one act of hypocrisy let us look at an episode that took place in Germany. There was a young Jewish boy who had a profound sense of admiration for his father. The life of the family centered around the acts of piety and devotion prescribed by their religion. The father was zealous in attending worship and instruction and demanded the same from his children. While the boy was a teenager the family was forced to move to another town in Germany. In the new location there was no synagogue and the pillars of the community all belonged to the Lutheran church. Suddenly the father announced to the family that they were all going to abandon their Jewish traditions and join the Lutheran church. When the stunned family asked "why" the father explained that it was necessary to help his business. The youngster was bewildered and confused. His deep disappointment soon gave way to anger and a kind of intense bitterness that plagued him throughout his life.

He left Germany and went to England to study. He sat daily at the British Museum formulating his ideas and composing a book. In that book he introduced a whole life and world view and conceived of a movement that was designed to change the world. In the book he described religion as an "opiate for the masses" that could be explained totally in terms of economics. Today there are two billion people in the world who live under the system invented by this embittered man. His name, of course, is Karl Marx. The influence of his father's hypocrisy is still being keenly felt around the world.

The church is not the only place where the effects of hypocrisy are felt. Fraud or the lie of any kind are forms of hypocrisy. When you pad your expense account you are practicing hypocrisy. When you twist the figures a bit on your income tax form, you are practicing hypocrisy. When you cheat on an examination in school, you are giving a fraudulent account of your knowledge to the professor.

There is a real sense in which all of us are hypocrites to some degree. When we seek to present a public image of ourselves that is better than we are, we play the game of the hypocrite.

The ultimate issue about Christianity is the person and work of Christ. The real question we must ask is, "Was Christ a hypocrite?" If Christ was a hypocrite then there is no reason at all to become involved with His church. But if He was not a hypocrite, but was everything He claimed to be, then we must be committed to His church. The purpose of the church is not to bring praise and honors to its members. The church exists to honor and obey Christ.

Christianity presents a perfect Christ for imperfect people. In Christ there is no deception. In Him there is no dishonesty, no fraud. He loved the truth; He did the truth; and He is the truth.

Key Points to Remember

1. *Hypocrisy in particular is not to be confused with sin in general.* Because all Christians sin does not mean that all Christians are hypocrites. There are hypocrites in the church, but the church is not "full of hypocrites."

2. *All Christians are sinners but not all Christians are hypocrites.* The church is full of sinners because the church was established as a refuge for sinners. One must be a sinner in order to be a member of the church.

3. *Hypocrisy, as a fraud, does exist in the church.* It is a serious sin. There are hypocrites in the church who

pretend to be more righteous than they are. Hypocrisy takes many forms in the church. It is especially noticeable with respect to membership vows and marriage vows.

4. Clergy are not exempt from the sin of hypocrisy.

5. Jesus was sharply critical of the sin of hypocrisy, especially in the clergy of His day—the scribes and Pharisees. Ministers can become ordained for corrupt reasons. They also face enormous pressure to exhibit a higher level of righteousness than they have attained. No minister can fully "practice what he preaches" if he preaches the whole counsel of God.

6. Hypocrisy can have long-range damaging effects on people. Hypocrisy evokes disillusionment, anger and bitterness. The experience of Karl Marx is a key illustration of this.

7. Christ was not a hypocrite. The ultimate question of hypocrisy must be focused on Christ. Though people often judge Christianity by what Christians do, the final verdict must be about Christ Himself. Christianity offers the perfect Christ for imperfect people.

SIX

"I Don't Need Religion."

"Religion is a crutch for people who are not strong enough to cope with the pressures of life." "I don't feel the need for religion; my life is going smoothly." "Why can't you stand on your own two feet?"

Statements like these are uttered frequently in our society. People reflect not so much an attitude of hostility to Christianity, but rather a sense of indifference to any personal relevance of Christianity to their lives. Along with indifference is an element of puzzlement about why Christianity places so much emphasis on "grace" and religious activity. Often we hear people say, "I don't see why I can't satisfy God by just living a good life, doing my duty as a responsible citizen, avoiding gross and criminal acts, and by being kind to my neighbor. Why do I have to be religious? Why should I act

pious with expressions of repentance and prayer and all
the right 'religious' moves?"

These questions do not waste time with idle criticisms
aimed at the periphery of Christianity, but they go to the
core of what Christianity is all about. The essence of
theology is grace, and without an understanding of it we
cannot possibly understand what Christianity is.

What's the Matter with Humanism?

A major factor which causes difficulty in understanding the Christian emphasis on grace can be seen in the
heavy influence generated on our culture by the philosophy of humanism.

Humanism as an "ism" manifests itself under several
different varieties. All forms of it, however, place great
stress on the value if mankind's virtues such as honesty,
industry, justice, charity, and others are extolled as
prerequisites for the general welfare of mankind. The
humanist will often be engaged in heroic acts of self-
sacrifice to advance the cause of human dignity and
freedom. At certain points it is easy to confuse Christianity with humanism because Christianity is also deeply concerned about values and virtue and the welfare of
mankind. The basic point of difference, however,
focuses on their respective evaluations of the moral ability of man. The humanist recognizes that man is not
perfect. He knows that people are capable of committing
all sorts of cruel and atrocious acts. Yet the humanist
remains convinced that evil is something that is only a
defect that mars man on the surface. The humanist has
confidence that the heart of man is basically good. As
long as a person achieves a certain standard of virtue, he
need not be dependent upon religious means to excuse
his failures to achieve these virtues. Self-discipline and
effort are called for instead of a pious posture of prayer

and fasting. "God helps those who help themselves" is the motto of the humanist.

A classic expression of the humanist approach to virtue may be found in the *Autobiography of Benjamin Franklin*. Franklin relates how at one point in his life he resolved to begin a rigorous program of moral self-improvement. He wrote out a morality grid by which he was able to monitor his daily progress in his effort to achieve high levels of honesty, humility, charity, frugality, and a host of other virtues. He gives at times a humorous account of the pitfalls and frustrations he encountered in his pilgrimage. He had a particularly difficult time wrestling with humility. If, for example, Franklin discovered that he had done well in cultivating humility for three days in a row, he became proud of his progress. Then he realized that the more success he had in his pursuit of humility the more proud he was actually becoming!

A constant problem faced by the humanist is the problem of the downward spiral of adjustments of moral expectation. If we cling to the idea that man is basically good, we must relativize the standard of goodness and reduce it to a low level in order to keep the myth alive. The standard of "goodness" must be low enough that the average person can meet it consistently. It is precisely at this point that humanism is on a collision course with Christianity.

Isn't "Trying to Do the Right Thing" Enough?

The conflict between Christianity and humanism is a conflict of ultimate standards. Christianity evaluates the performance of mankind not by national averages or a low common denominator of human behavior. Goodness is not defined by statistical normalcy. Christianity asserts that normal man is fallen man. The standard of goodness is found in the holiness of God. Christianity takes seriously the divine mandate, "Be holy, for I am holy" (Lev. 14:44; see also 1 Pet. 1:16). Man's role as the image-bearer of God carries with it an awesome moral responsibility that cannot be neutralized by a relative standard of goodness.

The problem of relativized standards can be seen vividly in Jesus' encounter with the rich young ruler (see Luke 18:18 ff). The young man approaches Jesus with a spirit of enthusiasm asking, "Good Teacher, what shall I do to inherit eternal life?" Note carefully the response of Jesus. He does not accept the flattery of the young man by saying, "Thank you very much for acknowledging my goodness." Rather, He gives a somewhat startling reply, "Why do you call me good? No one is good but God alone" (v. 19). Jesus offers a rebuke to the man for his casual use of the word "good." The point of Jesus' reply is not to deny His own deity or His own sinlessness. (The young man surely was not aware of the full identity of Christ.) The point of Jesus' remarks is to challenge the assumptions about goodness the young man had. He says to the youth, "You know the commandments: 'Do not commit adultery, Do not kill, Do not steal, Do not bear false witness, Honor your father and mother.' " The young man quickly replied, "All these have I observed from my youth" (vv. 20,21).

"All these have I observed from my youth." Think of that statement. Within the breast of the rich young ruler beat the heart of a thorough-going humanist. He actually believed that he had kept the moral law of God throughout his entire life. His unspoken thought was obviously, "Oh, is that all I have to do? Well, I must be in pretty good shape to inherit eternal life." It is probable that the young man was not present when Jesus preached the sermon on the mount. In that sermon

Jesus elaborated the broader implications of the moral law of God. The young man probably didn't realize that if he had lusted after a woman, he had violated the broader dimensions of the prohibition against adultery. He probably didn't realize that if he hated his brother, he had violated the broader application of the prohibition against murder. He had preserved himself from the more gross and crass violations of the law and therefore thought that his record was clean. In a word, he had adjusted the demands of the law downward.

Jesus' response was somewhat subtle and indirect. He didn't argue with the man by saying, "Oh no you didn't. You haven't kept these commandments since you got out of your bed this morning." Instead Jesus said to him, "One thing you still lack. Sell all that you have and distribute to the poor ... and come, follow me" (v. 22). Why did Christ change the whole conversation from goodness and law to money? I suspect the reason is obvious. Jesus started with the first commandment, "Thou shalt have no other gods before me," and put the ruler to the test. He couldn't even pass the test on the first commandment for we read, "But when he heard this he became sad, for he was very rich" (v. 23).

The issue of this encounter between Jesus and the rich man was not about money but goodness. The man wanted eternal life but he didn't want to be religious. He didn't want to depend on grace to gain that inheritance.

Don't We Have to Earn Our Way to Heaven?

If we ask why it is necessary for grace to be central to the Christian life, the answer is very simple: *Man is morally incapable of earning his way into the Kingdom of God. Man is not good enough to merit an eternal relationship with God.*

The New Testament makes it abundantly clear that

our noblest efforts at self-reformation or human virtue fall short of what God's holiness requires. The apostle Paul states it succinctly when he declares, "No flesh shall be justified by the works of the law" (see Rom. 3:20).

Not only does the New Testament make it clear that our feeble efforts at righteousness do not measure up to the demands of the law, but it adds the radical notion that we are morally incapable of doing what God requires. This is a "hard saying." In essence, the Bible says that we are not able to do what we are required to do. "The mind that is set on the flesh is hostile to God; it does not submit to God's law, indeed it cannot; and those who are in the flesh cannot please God" (Rom. 8:7). The New Testament describes us as being "flesh" by nature. That condition of flesh involves such a moral weakness that we cannot do what God requires.

But if we cannot, apart from grace, do what God requires, how can God possibly hold us responsible? How can He hold us accountable to a law we cannot keep? Keep in mind that the law requires perfection, yet none of us is perfect. How can God require perfection from imperfect creatures?

To understand this dilemma even in the slightest we must come to an understanding of the meaning of "cannot." In what sense are we unable to fulfill the law of God?

Theologians have wrestled with this "cannot" problem for centuries. Jonathan Edwards provides one distinction that is helpful. He distinguished between what he called man's "natural ability" and man's "moral ability." Natural ability means the necessary power or equipment to perform a task. For a being to do moral works he must have moral powers. He must have a will and a mind, for example. A creature without a will cannot make moral decisions. A creature without a mind cannot respond with understanding to moral concerns. Thus, for man to be able to be a moral creature, there is certain basic "equipment" necessary. If God commanded us to fly, we would not be able to comply, not on moral grounds but on natural grounds. We lack the ability to fly, not because we are sinners, but because God has not provided us with wings. Birds have the natural ability to fly but human beings do not. Man can only fly by artificial and mechanical means. Edwards would say, therefore, that if God required man to fly, He would be unjust in making such a demand because man lacks the natural ability to do it.

Man does have the natural ability to be morally perfect inasmuch as he has the necessary natural equipment to perform moral acts. Yet, the Bible says there is a sense in which man cannot do what he is required to do. Edwards calls this a "moral inability." Man has a mind and a will; but in order to exercise that mind and will to obedience, what else would man need to have? He would have to have some kind of inner disposition or inclination toward God. In simple terms, he would need to have a "desire" to please God. Edwards maintains that when the New Testament says that man cannot keep the law of God, it is not because he lacks a will or a mind and cannot understand what God requires, but rather because man does not have a proper disposition toward God. Man, in his fallenness, is in a state of enmity and estrangement from God. The Scriptures tell us that the desires of man's heart are wicked continually. The Bible acknowledges that man has a will, but that will is "under the power" of sin and in "bondage" to sin.

What Good Is Having a Free Will?

Edwards' distinction between natural and moral ability touches heavily on the classic issue of free will. Does Christianity teach that man has a free will? How can we be in bondage to sin and have a free will at the same time? These questions are inseparably related to the question of why we need grace. They touch the point of deepest conflict between Christianity and humanism.

If by nature I am in bondage to sin and my will is morally unable to obey God, how can I still be held responsible? These questions have far-reaching implications that are well beyond the scope of this book, but some foundational matters of the will must be briefly discussed.

Christian scholars from Augustine to Luther and Calvin to the present have consistently maintained that fallen man indeed has a free will, but their understanding of "free will" is different from that of the humanist. Augustine, for example, argued that man has a free will, but he does not have liberty. Calvin argued that man has a free will but is in bondage to sin. At first glance these statements from theologians sound contradictory. What do they mean by these assertions?

To simplify the matter, what the theologians mean is that man is free insofar as he is able to choose what he wants to choose. To go a step farther, they would maintain that not only can man choose what he wants to choose, but that he always does in fact choose what he wants to choose. To be free is to be able to choose what you want. This, in fact, is what we always do. Sometimes it seems like that is not the case. There are times when it seems we are forced to act against our desires. For example, if a thief were to come up to me and point a pistol at me and say, "Your money or your life," I would experience what we call "coercion." In such a situation my freedom would be greatly curtailed and restricted but not altogether destroyed. The thief would reduce my options to two. All things being equal, I would probably not have a great desire to give the thief all of my money. But when my choices are reduced to two, and one of them is death, I do have a certain desire or inclination to hand over the money. Total coercion would occur if the thief stepped up to me, shot me dead, and helped himself to my money. Then my freedom would be as dead and inert as I would be.

The whole matter of making choices is very complex. Most of the time our choices are not limited to two. We have a whole network of desire factors at work within us. Often they are in conflict; rarely are they at a consistent level of intensity. Some days I have an intense desire to serve Christ and obey God. At other times, I am listless in my faith and not very zealous to obey God. But one thing remains constant: I always make my choices according to the strongest inclination I have at the moment of decision. For example, if my desire to obey God were always greater than my desire to sin, I would never sin. When I sin, on the other hand, it is because I want to sin more than I want to obey God. Nobody forces me though many may entice and encourage me to sin. It is precisely because I sin according to my desires that God holds me responsible for my action.

Two serious questions remain to be dealt with about the matter of freedom. In the first place, if it is true that I always act according to my strongest inclination and in fact I must choose according to my inclinations, doesn't that involve a kind of determinism? If my choices are controlled by my inclinations, can I be said to be really free? The answer to both of these questions is yes. Freedom does not involve a kind of determinism. But the determining factor in moral decisions is the self. This we call self-determination, which is the essence of freedom. Determinism as an "ism" is that theory which reduces man to the utter control and manipulation of forces external to himself. Self-determination stands over against external determinism.

The second question relative to the matter of choosing according to our strongest inclination is the question of why we have no positive inclination toward God. If we must have an inclination toward God before we can obey Him, and we lack such inclination, how can God hold us responsible? A moral disposition toward God in the final analysis, is as necessary to obedience as wings are to flying. We lack the desire to obey God, and consequently the Bible says we "cannot" obey Him. But how can we be held responsible? The biblical answer throws many for a loop. The Bible makes it clear that we are in fact held responsible for our very inability to obey God. We are judged guilty for our representative participation in the fall of Adam.

We are born in a corrupt state and yet are held responsible for being in that corrupt state. Yet, we are fallen not because of what we have done but because of what Adam did for us. This poses the very thorny theological problem of what is called "alien guilt." It raises the further question of God's holding me responsible for what somebody else did long before I was born. How can a just God do that?

Why Am I Blamed for Something I Didn't Do?

These issues are very difficult to treat in such a brief fashion, but a cursory glance at the problem may yield some helpful guidelines to further reflection. I understand to some degree how the law can hold me accountable for acts done by someone else. If I enter into a conspiracy with a hired assassin to murder someone, I can be charged with first degree murder. Though my hands never touch the gun and I am far removed from

96

the scene of the crime, I am considered as guilty as if I pulled the trigger myself. I am held accountable for what my hired representative did for me.

But who hired Adam? Can I not cry out to God, "No damnation without just and proper representation!"? I never entered into a conspiracy with Adam. Not only was I not at the scene of the crime, I wasn't even born yet. I may have been represented by Adam, but I had nothing to say about the selection of my representative. Suppose people requested of a king that they be represented and the king responded by appointing his own henchmen as the people's representatives. We would call that tyranny. The people would demand the right to vote for their own representatives. Why? The word "vote" comes from the Latin *votum* which has to do with choice and desire. I want to vote for my own representative so that I may be fairly represented.

Why do we want "fair" representation? We want to have some assurance that our representatives accurately represent us. If someone else appoints my representative, I have no safeguard that the representative will act in my best interests. On the other hand, even if I do have the right to choose my own representative, I have no guarantee that he would act out my choice. We all have experienced the frustration of being deceived by the campaign promises of elected officials which are never carried out.

Every time I choose a representative, my choice is a fallible one. Only once in all of history have I had an infallibly chosen representative. That was in Eden. To be sure, God made the choice for me; but I must face the question: "Was God's infallible choice of my representative a more accurate or less accurate choice than I could or would have made myself?" If we say that God's choice was anything less than a perfect one, we slander

His righteousness and only prove the accuracy of His selection. If I charge God with tyranny, assuming I would have done differently, I only manifest the corruption that Adam's fall brought me. Thus, I share with Adam in a corporate fall and a corporate guilt. My sinful disposition is my own fault, and I cannot blame it on Adam or on God.

The Christian believes that man is fallen but remains free to act according to his disposition. Because the disposition is corrupt, man lacks the moral ability to obey God. Only by grace can such a fallen creature be restored and redeemed. Without that grace, efforts of moral perfection are doomed to failure.

The humanist has a notion of freedom that differs sharply from the Christian view. Humanistic notions of freedom tend to view the heart of man as being in a state of moral neutrality. The popular notion is this: When confronted by a moral decision I have the power to do the good or not to do the good. There is no predisposition that controls my choice either to good or to evil. My choices are utterly spontaneous. According to the humanist, predisposition destroys freedom. According to Christianity, the absence of predisposition would destroy freedom.

Suppose I were confronted by a choice but had absolutely no inclination to either the good or the bad; which would I choose? Why would I choose it? More importantly *how* could I choose either. My choice would be an effect without a cause which is irrational. If there would be no reason for my choice, my choice would be utterly arbitrary and have no moral value. The humanist has a twofold problem. He cannot account for a "spontaneous" choice in the first place, and even if such an irrational act actually happened, he cannot give any moral significance to it.

Not only does reason militate against the humanist notion of freedom, but history gives him problems as well. If man is born in a state of moral neutrality, how can we account for the universality of human imperfection? Surely some percentage of persons would be able to make it through life without sinning. There would be no reason why anyone would ever sin, not to mention the majority or, worse yet, everybody. The most frequent response to this, which unfortunately reflects a somewhat shallow level of thinking, is that because society is corrupt and morally innocent people are raised in such a corrupt environment, eventually everyone gets tainted by sin. The superficiality of this line of reasoning may be seen by merely asking the question, "How did society become corrupt in the first place?" Why are there no morally perfect societies or even societies where half of the people are perfect? Diogenes' quest for the honest man continues to this day. If the Bible never mentioned original sin, we could easily postulate it from a study of history and human society.

Why Do I Need Grace?

Why is grace necessary? For liberation and reconciliation with God. Without grace I am left with my fallenness and must face the judgment of God on the basis of my own performance.

The idea of a last judgment is not a popular one in our culture. The preaching of hell, fire, and damnation is no longer in vogue. A prevailing notion is that all we have to do to enter the Kingdom of God is to die. God is viewed as being so "loving" that He really doesn't care too much if we don't keep His law. The law is there to guide us, but if we stumble and fall, our celestial grandfather will merely wink and say, "Boys will be boys." We expect God to look at us (or overlook us), wink and smile tolerantly saying, "Oh well, nobody's perfect."

We face the problem of immunity to holiness by virtue of our comaraderie with sin. Since we are all imperfect, we consider that imperfection as being important. We expect that if God will hold us accountable for our lives that He will grade us on a curve. Our sins are many but they are not too serious, and God would certainly never punish us for them. These assumptions are both dangerous and ill-advised. One reason why we fail to see the urgency of the need of grace is because we operate with a totally different value system from that of God. Suppose we were called upon to establish 10 ultimate laws by which a nation should be governed. How many of us would include in the list an absolute command to honor parents? How many would include a law against coveting another person's property? How many would include a weighty prohibition against using the name of God in vain? Our priorities and values simply do not match those of God.

To state the conflict of values another way, let us consider the most important moral duty there is. God tells us that the *great commandment* is to love the Lord our God with all of our heart, soul, mind and strength and to love our neighbors as much as we love ourselves. This commandment is awesome. Whom do you know that loves God with all of his heart? How about all of the mind? Do we have a consummate passion to know God and to study His Word with rigorous diligence? Whom do you know who loves every person in the world as much as he loves himself? I know I haven't loved God with my whole heart for 60 seconds in my life.

Nobody keeps the great commandment. So what's the big deal? If no one abides by that particular law, it can't be that important. Yet God calls it the *great commandment.* What if he considers the breaking of that law as the *great transgression*? What if we are judged ultimately by that law? Would we need grace then?

Consider the implications of the great commandment. Is the law a good one? Suppose we all kept it perfectly. All jealousy, dishonesty, theft, and violence would disappear from the earth. No one would ever cheat, slander, or oppress his fellowman. God would be honored in all places. Justice and love would be universal. Failure to keep this law does not merely mean the loss of a utopian society, it means that we are guilty of nothing less than cosmic treason. Our slightest sins are acts of rebellion against the Creator of heaven and earth. At that point we defiantly refuse to submit to His authority or His rule. God takes that personally and He takes it very seriously.

But we have a safety valve. We will not become unduly alarmed as we contemplate the law of God. We know that God is a God of love and wouldn't let any of us perish in the end.

Now we are talking about grace. We have heard that God is gracious and thus there is nothing to worry about. I guess we do need grace, but I still don't have to be religious since God gives that grace to everyone. He must give that grace to everyone because He is a loving God. Loving gods don't allow anyone to perish. Does not love require that God give His grace to everyone equally in the end? This assumption is the most perilous assumption anyone could ever make about grace.

Though God's grace is plenteous and truly amazing, though His grace is freely given and is majestic in scope, it must never be taken for granted. Nothing requires that God be gracious, not even His love. If grace is ever required, it is no longer grace. Grace cannot be required. If we merit it then it is no longer grace; if God is obliged to give it then it is no longer grace. When we think that

God must be gracious, we confuse grace with justice. The most fearful mistake we could make would be to think in the deepest chambers of our hearts that somehow God "owes" us His grace. When we begin to think like this, it is time to go back and examine the law. Once I rebel against God, He owes me nothing. I desperately need His grace and will surely perish without it, but I can never demand that He give it to me.

We do not need to be religious in the sense of wearing certain clothes or using certain religious cliches or by affixing a certain saccharin smile to our faces. But we do need to be religious in the sense of depending fully on God's grace and making diligent use of the means of grace He provides for us. Repentance and faith are not unnecessary options with God. His grace comes with demands. For one who has experienced the grace of forgiveness those demands become opportunities for a display of gratitude. Our response to grace is obedience. The motive for obedience is not to enter the Kingdom but to honor the King who has already granted us access into His Kingdom. The sum of theology is grace. The sum of ethics is gratitude.

Key Points to Remember

1. The humanist doesn't need religion because he is confident that the heart of man is basically good. Even though humanism as an "ism" shares many common values with Christianity, the humanistic concept of "good" is on a collision course with Jesus' view of "good." The humanist's standard of goodness must be low enough for the average person to be able to meet it consistently. God's standard of goodness is perfection.

2. The rich young ruler failed in his quest for salvation because he was "good." He didn't want to depend on grace to gain that inheritance. Jesus tried to tell the young man that he had *not* kept all the commandments all the time, all his life. He proved this by asking the rich man to sell all his goods and follow Him—to obey the first commandment, "Thou shalt have no other gods before me." The young man could not do this. If he couldn't depend on his own righteousness for eternal life he didn't want it.

3. *God requires perfection from imperfect creatures.* We cannot be perfect because we do not have the "moral ability" to be perfect. We may have the "natural ability" because we have all the necessary equipment, but we are not morally inclined toward God.

4. *Man has free will—we can choose what we want.* We sin because we want to sin. We follow our strongest inclination at any given time.

5. *We are "responsible" for Adam's fall because Adam perfectly represented us.* We are born in a fallen state of corruption and bondage. Because we also are fallen we need grace.

6. *God never owes us grace.* Grace is not justice. If God deals with us ultimately on the basis of justice alone, we will perish.

seven

"There Is No God!"

We no longer live in an age where the existence of God is taken for granted. In former times people debated such questions as "What is God like?" or "How many gods are there?" That there was a god or gods was tacitly assumed by almost everyone. Times have changed. Our age has been called the age of skepticism. Belief in God is no longer considered necessary or, in some cases, even desirable. Christian thinkers do not dominate the world of philosophy as they once did. Christian art is no longer the focal point of cultural expressions.

Since the eighteenth-century period of the Enlightenment and the advent of the age of science, there has been a growing sentiment that clinging to a belief in God is an option for those who cannot face living in a universe where things happen by impersonal natural laws.

We have no firsthand evidence that can be scientifically measured about some being that lives "out there." The Soviet cosmonaut, Yuri Gagarin, commented after orbiting the earth, "I didn't see any God out there." God has not been discovered in a test tube or a telescope. Thus we are left with nonempirical means such as religious experience and emotional feelings to foster a belief in God. The prevailing mood is that science yields no evidence to support belief in God and in fact has presented evidence that makes belief in a god somewhat tenuous.

This climate of opinion that science has made God unnecessary or even untenable has left many people with a sense of agnosticism about the question. The most popular form of agnosticism found in our society is that which is nonmilitant. That is, people say, "We just don't have any compelling evidence to affirm the existence of God. There is not enough real knowledge to go on about a question like this."

Is the agnostic correct? Has science progressed to the point of being able to explain life and the universe adequately without reference to God? Does belief in God rest on emotion alone? As a theist I would like to deal with these questions. I would like to offer some evidence for the existence of God that deals with the issue in its most basic form.

Can You Prove God Exists?

Whatever else the Christian affirms about God, he affirms that God is the Creator of the world. God is said to exist of Himself and is eternal. Is such a notion of God reasonable? Is there any evidence to support such a view?

Let us begin our inquiry at the most basic point. Let's start by assuming that *something exists*. This is merely

105

a starting point for our inquiry. Some may object at the outset that we cannot prove that anything exists. Maybe all of reality is an illusion. Even the illusion is an illusion. Maybe there is no one having the illusion. For such people this argument will have no weight. But that's all right because such people don't even exist if nothing exists. My argument is addressed to people who do exist, and I will leave the objections to our initial assumption to the philosophers who must affirm my starting point in order to deny it. Where does our assumption lead us? I would like to show that if *something exists now, something has always existed.* Ah, there's the rub! It's one thing to affirm that something exists now, but that's a long way from asserting that something has always existed. Well, let's see how we get there.

If something exists now, we must affirm one of three things about it. It is either eternal, created by something that is eternal, or self-created. Can you think of any other alternatives? Which of these has been most frequently offered as an alternative by those who will not affirm the existence of God? The obvious answer is the third alternative. If we answer by either the first or the second, we have already affirmed that *something* is eternal (either an eternal world or an eternal creator). Only the third alternative gets us off the self-existent eternal hook. Let's take a closer look at it.

What About Creation by Chance?

During the period of the Enlightenment some of the French skeptics maintained that the God-hypothesis was no longer necessary because "now we know that the universe came into being by 'spontaneous generation.'" Spontaneous generation was a concept popular in the early days of the scientific revolution before advances were made in the scientific method of experimentation and observation. The sudden appearance of bacteria on bread or of tadpoles in a mud puddle was explained by spontaneous generation. Spontaneous generation means that something comes from nothing, and it is another way of saying self-creation. More careful scientists with better controlled experiments showed these theories to be wrong. Careful microscopic study revealed the sources of the bacteria and the tadpoles. In a short time the notion of spontaneous generation fell into disrepute and was scoffed at by scientists.

More recent versions of self-creation are expressed in more sophisticated terms. Now people speak of the origin of the universe in terms of quantum motion and combinations of space, time, and chance. In a popular sense this means "creation by chance." In spite of the new language that is used, these ideas remain expressions of the notion of self-creation.

What is wrong with the notion of self-creation? What would have to happen for something to create itself? Obviously, for something to create itself, it would have to exist in order to create. It would have to exist before it existed if it were to create its own existence. Are you getting a headache? For something to create itself it would have to be and not be at the same time and have the same relationship. To do that it would have to violate the law basic to all science, the law of contradiction. To say that something exists and does not exist at the same time and in the same way is to make a nonsense statement. The notion of self-creation is irrational in the extreme.

But what about creation by chance? To understand the problems with this idea we need a clear understanding of what chance is. Webster defines chance as "something that happens as the result of unknown or unconsidered forces." Chance describes a mathematical relationship of factors. To illustrate this, let's consider the matter of flipping a coin. We say that the chances of its coming up heads or tails are 50 percent. (That is, if we can keep it from sticking in the dirt and standing on edge.) Suppose the coin is flipped and comes up heads. What made it come up heads? Did chance do it? Of course not. Chance merely tells us the possibilities in light of a multitude of variables. We don't usually control all the elements that are involved in the flipping of a coin. When someone flips a coin we usually don't know whether it started with the head up, how much pressure was exerted by the thumb, how dense the atmosphere was into which it was flipped, or how many revolutions the coin made in the air. If we knew all of those factors with certainty we would welcome the opportunity to wager on the outcome at 2-1 odds.

What is the point of the analogy? Simply that chance has no power to cause anything. It has no power because it is nothing (that is no thing or no being). Chance is a mathematical abstraction with no real existence. Since it is nothing, it cannot do anything. To say that the world was created by chance is to say that it was created by nothing or was "self-created." Call it spontaneous generation or call it chance, but a rose by any other name—

Some scholars have used the expression "creation by chance" in a more accurate way. That is, they have followed Webster's definition and said, "We do not know how the universe came into being. Chances are it was this or chances are it was that. We just don't know." But that is not to say that the world came by chance in the sense that chance was the causal power. What are the chances that the universe was created by the power of chance? Not a chance.

If chance-creation means self-creation and is therefore illogical, does that mean it couldn't happen? Must reality be logical? Doesn't the quantum theory and the so-called "Heisenberg Indeterminacy Principle"[1] indicate that this is precisely what happens? We are faced with a language problem that involves a subtle but serious misuse of words.

Because the motion of atomic particles under certain experimental conditions appears unpredictable or "random," their behavior has been called indeterminate. What does that mean? Indeterminate is defined as "not determinate; indefinite; not distinct or precise; vague." To be indeterminate is not to be nondeterminate. Indeterminacy simply means that we don't know why the particles behave the way they do. That is not the same as saying that their motion is caused by nothing or by chance. To say that the motion is caused by nothing is to make a nonscientific and irrational statement.

To abandon the notion of God in light of the option of self-creation is intellectual suicide. It may be a popular idea socially but it cannot withstand even a rudimentary intellectual critique.

If we cannot appeal to self-creation as an explanation for what exists, then we must admit that something is eternal. We are still left with two possibilities: A self-existent eternal being who creates the world, or else an eternal world. Why not an eternal world? Those who have rejected the God-hypothesis and have seen the futility of the notion of self-creation have argued for the notion of an eternal world.

What About the Eternal World Option?
One Christian philosopher once wrote, "In the beginning matter created the heaven and the earth." And he then asked, "What is the matter with that?" He replied, "The matter with that is matter." What he was driving

at was that all of the observable characteristics of matter indicate that it is a dependent stuff. It changes, undergoes growth and manifests contingency. These notions are incompatible with the notion of eternality. But the objection is raised immediately, "Our knowledge of the material world is incomplete. Maybe there is a special part of the yet undiscovered material universe that is eternal and is the source or wellspring from which everything else comes." Perhaps that is a possibility. But then we would have to distinguish that part of the universe which is eternal and self-existent from the rest of the universe which would be its created creature. At least part of the universe would be transcendent to the other part, at least with respect to the character of its being. Yet this transcendence of being is precisely what we are pleading for with our notion of God.

What about a universe in process that involves the old idea of "an infinite series of finite causes"? Passing over the obvious difficulty with this idea, the first cause in this infinite chain, let us examine it more closely. Suppose there were some first cause in the series that was not self-existent (an irrational idea itself). What would happen if that being generated another similar being and then the first being died? If the first being passed out of existence then it obviously would not be eternal. But the universe would continue in the second being which now causes a third being and then itself passes out of existence. How does this process come about? Does the first being pass on some seminal part of its own being to the second one, and so on? If so, then the first being still has a continuing element that transcends the second being. If the process is not by some stable part of the original being, then perhaps it was accomplished by fiat. (Now that first being is beginning to show even more similarities to God.) Don't forget that we still have the massive problem of accounting for the first being referred to.

Some have maintained that it is not necessary to account for the first being because we are talking about an *infinite* series and, by definition, an infinite series has no first in the series. The concept of an infinite series of abstract numbers is one thing, but a series of real beings is something else. We still must talk of a first "being."

Others have maintained that the infinite series idea is defensible on the grounds that, in some cases, the whole can be greater than the sum of its parts. The illustration may be seen in Rembrandt's famous painting, *The Night Watch. The Night Watch* is a magnificent painting composed of individual brush strokes and pigment on a canvas. The total, however, is a work of art. We could take those same strokes, pigments, and pieces of canvas and rearrange them into a hideous and grotesque form. Hence the whole is "greater" than its parts. Again we have a word problem here. The word "greater" undergoes a subtle shift in meaning. Could we add up all the pigment, strokes, and canvas and come up with a live elephant? Certainly not. If we have 50 pounds of paint in the painting, can the fact that the paint is arranged in a beautiful way make the paint weigh 55 pounds? Thus, the concept of a real infinite series of finite causes is a meaningless concept.

What Is the Logic in a Self-Existent God Concept?

If self-creation is an absurd idea, why isn't self-existence equally absurd? If we examine these two concepts by the canons of logical, formal analysis, we can see they are quite different. As we have pointed out, the concept of self-creation involves a clear contradiction. To create itself something would have to be and not be at the same time and in the same relationship. On the other hand, for something to exist eternally in and of itself involves no contradiction. The notion of self-creation cannot pass the test of logic. The notion of self-existence violates no rule of logic and is not falsified by reason.

But doesn't Christianity teach that God created the world "out of nothing"? If God can create the world out of nothing, why can't the universe create itself out of nothing? Isn't there a basic axiom which says *ex nihilo nihil fit*—"out of nothing, nothing comes"? There is a crucial difference between God's creating something out of nothing and something creating itself out of nothing. To be sure, in both cases there is no material cause for the world. But with God we have an *efficient* cause; with self-creation, there is no *efficient* cause. How God creates is baffling and mysterious. But the idea of an eternal Being creating out of His own power with no material to use violates no rule of logic.

The law of causality. Doesn't the law of cause and effect apply to God as well as to the world? If everything must have a cause then who caused God? Aren't we being arbitrary by stopping our questions of cause when we get to God?

The confusion here rests with the statement "everything must have a cause." That is an incorrect phrasing of the law of causality. The law of cause and effect states simply that for every effect there is a cause. (An "effect" by definition is something that requires a cause.) God does not have a cause because He is eternal and self-existent. Being eternal, He is not an effect. Since He is not an effect He does not require a cause. He is uncaused. It is important to note the difference between an uncaused, self-existent eternal being and an effect that causes itself through self-creation!

An impersonal force or a personal God? Even if we grant that there must be something eternal and self-existent which is not the world as we know it, why can't it be some mysterious, impersonal force or, again, the infinite series? From whence comes the life out of this impersonal force? This is a particularly complicated problem because of the difficulty we have in defining life. If life is something special that can be distinguished from matter, then we must face the question of its origin. Can that which is not life produce life? This question deserves the same treatment as the original question of accounting for the "something" that is. If life is an effect, we must account for its cause. If matter is utterly lifeless, how can it produce life?

Even if it were conceivable for inanimate matter to produce life, could it produce intelligence if it were not intelligent itself? Intelligent life is life that has the ability to think and to act in a purposeful way. Can nature do that without intelligence? Can we have purpose by accident? Can we have intention unintentionally? If we say there is no purpose to the eye except that which accidentally developed (to provide sight) why should we call sight purposeful? If there is no purpose for the purpose, then the purpose is not really a purpose.

What we are getting at here is that the whole realm of nature shouts of the design of the universe. This design must have a designer or it is improper to call it design. Even Immanuel Kant in his vast critique of the traditional arguments for the existence of God was awed by the obvious presence of design in nature. Without the assumption of design in nature there can be no science. Even the evolutionist who wants to replace God with grand scale evolution must assume some sort of design to explain his theory of evolution.

If we discover that our self-existent eternal something is intelligent, then we know that he is also in some sense personal. He may be superpersonal, but he cannot be impersonal.

The argument from meaning. Since rational argumentation for the existence of God has gone out of style, many believers have turned their attention to construct "existential" arguments. These arguments have a greater element of raw emotion and subjective concern within them but are, nevertheless, valuable. The arguments run as follows: "If I am a result of a cosmic accident and my destiny is to be annihilated, how can I possibly have any significance in the meantime? If my origin is nothing and my destiny is nothing, how can my life be anything more than something that is, in Shakespeare's words, 'full of sound and fury, signifying nothing.' My life would be a 'tale told by an idiot.' " Here is where the emotional element enters. Every fiber of our being screams to us that we are significant and that our lives have meaning. Is there any more universal human aspiration than the aspiration to significance?

Less emotionally-oriented people might respond to this by saying, "Of course we would like to have significance and meaning, but let's face it, we can't say we have significance just because we want it." Here the critique of the nihilist is loud and clear. The nihilist says there is no meaning and life is ultimately an exercise in absurdity.

From a theoretical viewpoint the nihilist has a strong argument against anyone who rests his case for the existence of God on the grounds of human aspirations to significance. The nihilist must be answered by other arguments, such as those mentioned earlier. The value of the argument from meaning is its ability to expose the real issues and stakes of the God question.

The argument from meaning exposes the "eat your cake and have it too" philosophies that fall between full-bodied theism and radical nihilism. It exposes the intellectual bankruptcy of naturalistic humanism. Natu-

114

ralistic humanism maintains that man came from nothing and is going to nothing but meanwhile is full of significance. Virtues such as honesty and industry are exalted; human values such as liberation, civil rights, and health care are extolled. But from a theoretical perspective we must ask, "Why bother with human rights if man is ultimately insignificant. Who cares if black cosmic accidents have less rights than white cosmic accidents?" Such philosophy is rooted in sentiment and sentiment alone. The sentiment is great, to be sure, but we are still faced with the question of the nihilist, "If there is no God, why should man be thought important?"

It is not by accident that since the Enlightenment's rejection of God, the dominant theme of philosophy has been the question of the significance of man. We live in a time of genuine crisis about our own human identity. If we again open the question of the evidence of the existence of God, perhaps we may even discover that our aspirations to significance are not in vain.

Though many welcomed the "liberation" from the God-hypothesis that came with the skepticism of the Enlightenment, later thinkers have become less enthusiastic about the results of the liberation. Without the specter of God hanging over our heads, nineteenth-century man looked forward to the freedom of creating his own destiny. The marvelous advances of science and technology gave a ground basis for optimism. The optimism soon turned to pessimism when man began to contemplate the fuller implications of a godless universe. Without God man has no reference point to define himself. Twentieth-century philosophy manifests the chaos of man seeking to understand himself as a creature with dignity while having no reference point for that dignity.

Key Points to Remember

"There is no God!" In this age of skepticism, belief in God is no longer considered necessary or, in some cases, even desirable. The evidence for the existence of God must begin with creation.

1. Something cannot come from nothing. The oldest and best evidence for the existence of God is the evidence of the world itself. From sophisticated technical arguments offered by philosophers to the simple awareness of an uneducated person it is clear that the world had to be caused by something.

2. The words "chance" and "spontaneous generation" are empty terms. People play with these words in an attempt to disclaim God as Creator. Spontaneous generation or creation by chance cannot withstand even a rudimentary intellectual critique.

3. If something exists now something has always existed. Self-existence means that something has the power, within itself, of being. This power is eternal and presents no rational difficulty. Self-creation is irrational because for something to create itself *it must be before it is.*

4. The God of the Bible is self-existent and eternal. God created the world out of nothing (see Ps. 104:5-9; Job 38:4,5; Heb. 11:3).

5. The world exhibits design. This design must have a designer or it is improper to call it design.

Note

1. The scientific principle for the apparent behavior of atomic particles under certain conditions.

"If There Is a God Why Is There So Much Evil in the World?"

If God is perfect, how can there be evil in the world? Beyond the question of suffering we must face the question of how we account for the presence of wickedness in the world. The question of the origin of evil has been called the "Achilles heel" of Christianity. This vulnerable point has been the subject of considerable philosophical speculation and criticism.

The force of the question can be illustrated by the dilemma posed by many critics such as John Stuart Mill. The dilemma is frequently stated as follows:

> If God desires there to be evil in the world, then He is not good. If He does not desire there to be evil, yet evil exists, then He is not omnipotent. Thus, if evil exists God is either

not loving or not all-powerful. Evil casts a shadow over God's love and power. This is no small dilemma, and answers to it are exceedingly difficult.

Attempts to answer the dilemma posed by Mill and others have taken the form of the "theodicy." A theodicy is a rational attempt to explain how God can be just and still allow evil in the world. The word comes from a compound Greek root: *Theos* (God) *dikos* (just). The goal of the theodicy is to exonerate God from all blame and culpability for evil.

Is Evil Really Good in Disguise?

Frequent attempts at theodicy have tried to argue that what appears to be evil is in the final analysis really good. Evil only seems to be evil from a temporal perspective but in God's eternity is really good. The classic biblical reference offered in support of such a theodicy is the text, "All things work together for good for those who love Him" (see Rom. 8:28). Such an inference drawn from the text is gratuitous. The text does not assert that "all things are good" but that they work together for good for a limited number of people (those who love God). This text does assert God's triumph over evil, His ability to redeem evil, and His ability to bring good out of evil. But evil out of which God brings good is real evil. From the betrayal of Jesus by Judas comes the redemptive act of the cross, but that in no way minimizes the wickedness of Judas' act.

The "evil is good" theodicy fails because it obscures the real difference between good and evil. It is an implicit denial of the reality of evil. Even worse, it commits the error, indeed the sin, which the Bible typifies as a characteristic of wickedness, namely the calling of evil good and, by implication, the good, evil.

Does Evil Come from Satan?

Another common theodicy is found in the notion of an ultimate dualism. Dualism postulates the existence of two ultimate opposing forces which are equal in power and eternality. This view gets God off the hook by making the existence of evil eternally independent of Him. It resolves Mill's dilemma by submerging the one pole under the other. God's goodness is maintained at the cost of His omnipotence. Dualism limits God's power eternally. This theory ascribes the origin of evil to an eternal "devil" who is a god in his own right.

Such a view causes grave problems for the Christian because it excludes the possibility of redemption of evil. If evil is equal in power to God, God has no way to overcome it. With dualism there is no guarantee of redemption, nor even the possibility of it.

From another perspective, dualism has problems of a different kind. It fails to explain the origin of evil on rational grounds. If we have two ultimate opposing forces which are equal in power and are mutually exclusive and contradictory, how can we have anything? It is the rational problem of the irresistible force and the immovable object. What happens if we posit the theory of the meeting of an absolutely immovable object with an absolutely irresistible force? If the immovable object moves then it is not immovable. If it does not move, the irresistible force is resistible! It is rationally absurd to have two absolute, mutually exclusive entities. Even if it were hypothetically possible (which it is not) it could not account for real manifestations of good or evil. We would have a universe paralyzed by ultimate moral inertia. Absolute evil would always be checked by absolute good. Absolute good would always be checked by absolute evil. In this scheme neither good nor evil would be possible.

119

Do We Have to Have Evil to Appreciate Good?

A third type of theodicy is found in the theory that a temporary experience of evil is necessary or conducive to an ultimate appreciation of the good. This argument, which has been given in very sophisticated forms, has a great popular following. The argument contends that to appreciate health, I must first experience sickness; to appreciate righteousness, I must first experience wickedness. The argument seems weighty inasmuch as we do experience the intensity of appreciation by way of such contrasting experiences. I do appreciate health more fully after I've recovered from a serious illness or a painful injury. But the theodicy has its problems. If the experience is *necessary* for the appreciation of good then God Himself must experience evil for Him to appreciate the good. If it is not necessary, but merely conducive to the appreciation of the good, then we fall back into the first theodicy. This would simply mean that evil is ultimately good. All the problems of the first theodicy would be repeated here plus the added ethical questions of the end justifying the means.

Isn't Evil Relevant?

A fourth type of theodicy is that which explicitly denies the reality of evil. Other theodicies do it subtly and by logical implication. But this theodicy does it in bold type. It is not even properly called a theodicy because it doesn't seek to justify God but to eliminate Him (at least as a moral being). This approach maintains that there is no such thing as good or evil, only social convictions or preferences that masquerade as real values. Statements like, "Nothing is good or evil; only how you feel about it matters," are commonplace. The immediate question is, "How can it matter how you feel about it then?" When we speak of things mattering, we are talking again about values. If we value anything, we are talking about good and evil.

The above can be illustrated by relating a brief conversation I had with a devotee of Christian Science. Though believing in the reality of good, he contended that evil is just an illusion. There is really no evil. I asked the man if he thought it was good that I was teaching people that evil was real. He said, "No." I asked him if it was evil that I was teaching falsehood about evil. He had no answer. If he objected to my assertion of the reality of evil, he had to affirm my thesis in order to deny it. His only recourse was to treat me as an illusion. Frequently people argue that there is no good or evil or right or wrong. I have never heard anyone state the argument for five minutes without making assertions about right and wrong or good and evil in the process. This "theodicy" is what is commonly referred to as a "cop-out."

After All I'm Only Human!

One of the most sophisticated theodicies ever devised is that propounded by the philosopher Gottfried Leibniz. Leibniz differentiated between three kinds of evil. He distinguished between moral evil, physical evil, and metaphysical evil.

Leibniz defined moral evil in terms of acts performed by volitional beings. Creatures with understanding and wills have the ability to perform moral evil. Stones and flowers aren't moral creatures in this sense.[1] Physical evil is defined in terms of physical suffering brought about by disease, injury, or natural disasters like earthquakes. Metaphysical evil is related to the limitations of finitude or creatureliness.

It is this third category of "metaphysical evil" that is the heart of Leibniz's theodicy. To be anything less than metaphysically "perfect" is to be "evil." For example, if my knowledge is less than absolutely comprehensive, I suffer from metaphysical imperfection. Only an all-knowing, omniscient being would be metaphysically perfect. If I'm finite, I am incomplete and imperfect.

Leibniz's theory then proceeds to argue that ultimately both physical evil and moral evil "flow out" of metaphysical evil. In a word, we sin because we are finite. This is a novel expression of the old adage "to err is human." Thus, to be finite is to be *necessarily* evil.

How is God absolved of blame in all this? God is exonerated simply because He has done the best job He could do. He has created the "best of all possible worlds." Leibniz recognized that for God to create a metaphysically perfect world, He would have to create another God. Even God cannot create another God. God by definition is not a created being. If God tried to create another God, the second "god" would be a creature. The "god" would be dependent, derived, and finite. He simply could not qualify for the job description of being God.

But if God cannot create another God, doesn't that mean that God is not omnipotent? Again, Mill's dilemma seems to haunt Leibniz. Leibniz's God can still be good and loving because out of an infinite number of possible blueprints for a created world, God chose the best one. But if He were limited to imperfection, doesn't that mean there is something God cannot do, namely, create a perfect world? The answer is obvious. Yes, there is something God cannot do. In fact there are many things God cannot do. Reason tells us He cannot be God and not be God at the same time and in the same relationship. God cannot make a square circle or a two-sided triangle. Triangles by definition have three sides.

The point that is crucial, however, it that all of this

does not deny the omnipotence of God but affirms it. The point of confusion rests with the meaning of the term "omnipotence." As a theological term the word does not mean that God can do anything. What it does mean is that God does have all power over His creatures. The whole created order is always under the control and authority of God.

Leibniz's theodicy has impressed many and appears as a neat and clever argument. But the argument is filled with difficulties, especially for the Christian. There are both biblical and rational problems with it.

The biblical difficulty with Leibniz's theodicy focuses on the concept of an unavoidable fall of man. If moral evil flows out of metaphysical evil, then not only is God exonerated for evil but so is man. If man's sin is directly bound up with his creatureliness then it follows that he has no guilt. It would also mean that there is no hope of man's ultimate liberation from sin in heaven because he will still be a creature.

The chief rational objection to Leibniz's theodicy deals with his use of language. The basic fallacy of equivocation is not avoided by his definitions of different kinds of evil. The word "evil" when applied to finitude connotes something morally wrong; especially when moral evil is tied up with metaphysical evil, the changes of the meaning of "evil" become obscured. Though Leibniz does not like to speak of a causal connection between finitude and sin and prefers to speak of sin "flowing out of" finitude, the implication of causal necessity is there. If there is a necessary causal connection then moral evil cannot be called "sin." If there is no necessary causal relationship then the origin of evil has not been adequately explained. If sin does not *necessarily* flow from finitude then we must ask why in some cases it does and in others it does not.

Why Must I Suffer for What Adam Did?

Perhaps the most frequent theodicy offered by the Christian to the problem of evil is to ground the origin of evil in the free will of man. Man has the ability to sin because he is free. The strength of this argument is found in the fact that it reflects the biblical assertion that God is not the author of evil. Since the Bible clearly places the guilt and responsibility for sin on man, it seems natural to assume that sin comes with the power of freedom of choice.

However, the appeal to man's freedom as an answer to this question is not without its serious difficulties. Again the difficulties are of both a biblical and a rational kind.

The Bible tells us that sin entered the human experience by way of the fall of Adam and Eve. It tells us that they were created good and then fell by choosing to sin. The question is, how could something created good choose something evil. If we say Adam was deceived, we have two problems. In the first place the Bible makes it clear that Adam knew that what he was doing was wrong. Thus, the idea of innocent deception or sinning by ignorance are at odds with the text. The second problem is again the problem of guilt and responsibility. If Adam was deceived or ignorant of his actions, how could he be held guilty?

Perhaps Adam was coerced to sin. If he were forced to sin then freedom as an answer to our original dilemma is useless. The idea of coercion violates the biblical account and would absolve Adam of any responsibility.

What if Adam sinned because he had an evil inclination in his heart? That would explain how he was able to choose evil, but it would leave us with the thorny question of where he got the evil inclination in the first place. If God gave him the evil inclination, the responsibility for sin falls back to God. If God didn't give it to Adam, how did he acquire it?

What if all the inclinations of Adam's heart were only good ones? Then we still have the problem of asking how an evil choice would come from a good inclination.

The standard reply to these questions is that Adam had no inclinations either to the good or to the bad but rather had a moral disposition that was utterly neutral. This whole view of freedom of the will is treated more fully in the chapter on "I Don't Need Religion." The basic problem, however is this: If Adam has no inclination to sin or to good, how could he choose either one of them? Without desire or disposition, the will has no power to choose. Even if the will could act without inclination, would the choice be a moral one? If Adam chose evil for no reason or from no inclination or desire, the choice would be utterly arbitrary. In a word, it would be an accident with no moral responsibility attached.

These difficulties are why Karl Barth has called the fall of man an "impossible possibility." Why does he make such an utterly absurd statement? We must say sin is possible because it is actual. If Adam did sin, that is the clearest evidence that he could sin! But we can't figure out *how* he did it. Barth's clever statement of impossible possibility is not the remark of a stupid man. The statement is made not to explain the fall but to dramatize the rational problems connected with it. Barth uses startling language to underline the rational difficulty in explaining the fall.

Some search for the explanation for Adam's fall within the dimension of the influence of Satan. This approach simply removes the dilemma one step. All the difficulties raised with respect to the "how" of Adam's fall must then be faced with the question of the "how" of Satan's fall.

These theodicies are but a few of the more popular of the multitude of theories that have been offered as possible solutions to the enigma of sin. I am not satisfied with any of them. It is not my intent to be the devil's advocate or to lend assistance to those who reject Christianity because of these objections. I am not trying to give the skeptic more ammunition than he may already have. I am trying to make it clear that the problem is a severe one and one for which I have no adequate solution. I do not know how evil could originate with a good God. I am baffled by it, and it remains a troublesome mystery to me.

However, I am not prepared to jettison Christianity because of the mystery of evil. I think there is too much evidence for the existence of a good God and for the existence of real evil to abandon either assertion.

Though I cannot solve the dilemma of evil, I think it is still important to recognize other implications of the question that at least make the burden of the mystery a bit easier to bear.

What Is Evil?

Before any solution to the problem of evil can be found, we must deal with the question of the nature of evil. What is evil? How are we to describe it? What is the difference between good and evil?

The classical Christian philosophers Saint Augustine and Saint Thomas Aquinas both wrestled deeply with the problem of evil. Though their methods of doing philosophy differed sharply, they shared some similar ideas about the nature of evil. Through their influence some basic assumptions about evil were formulated.

Classically, evil is defined in terms of the Latin words *negatio* and *privatio*. That is, the notions of *negation* and *privation* are pivotal to the definition of evil. Negation refers to the negative ways in which evil is defined. When we talk about evil we tend to do it in negative terms. We speak of *un*righteousness, *un*godliness, *un*ethical, *ir*religious *dis*obedience and even *anti*-Christ. These prefixes have one thing in common: they involve the negation of the positive root of the word. Their meaning depends upon a prior understanding of the positive roots themselves. To understand what *un*righteousness is, we must first have some idea of what righteousness is. To understand what *in*-human behavior is, we must first understand what human behavior is. Our language betrays the fact that to think about and conceptualize evil, we must do it against the background of the good. Evil is understood over against the good. Thus evil is dependent, contingent, and derived from our understanding of good. Evil is spoken of as a negation of the good. It is dependent upon good for its own definition.

Along the same lines, evil is described in terms of privation. It refers to a lack or a want of the positive good. The Westminster Catechism, for example, defines sin as "any want of conformity to or transgression of the law of God." Here sin is defined as a lack of conformity to law or failure to be obedient. Sin is a privation of obedience, a law*less*ness.

These terms of negation and privation might bring with them the temptation to regard evil as being nonexistent. If it is merely the absence of something positive, maybe it is nothing at all. But these terms are not employed to lend credence to the notion that evil is illusory or impotent. Out of the Protestant Reformation came the added qualifier *actuosa*. Evil was defined as *privatio actuosa*. This meant that though evil is contingent and dependent, it is nevertheless real and powerful. The point is that evil cannot exist in and of itself. It depends

127

on the corruption of that which is good for its existence and power.

If all of this is true, how does it ease, for the Christian, the burden of Mill's dilemma? Though it does not eliminate the dilemma, it does make it a bit easier to bear. Why? Because though we are left with a serious unresolved problem, our situation is only half as bad as that of the unbeliever. The unbeliever not only has the problem of explaining the origin of evil, he has the problem of explaining the origin of good. It is only in light of the good that evil becomes a problem. We can account for the origin of good but not of evil. The pagan can account for the origin of neither. Thus, the reality of evil ironically gives indirect evidence for the existence of God.

To be sure, the atheist may counter by saying that he has no problem at all because good and evil are both nonexistent. He can say, and atheists have said, that all judgments of good and evil are arbitrary and thus ultimately meaningless. The option he chooses at this point is thoroughgoing nihilism. This option is a weighty one, but no one holds it consistently. The most radical nihilists continue to make value judgments as if they had meaning. They can't seem to escape some judgments of good and evil.

The existence of evil certainly doesn't prove the existence of God. If evil is real, however, it points to the good. Any refutation of nihilism must involve other arguments. It must be established on the basis of positive arguments for the existence of God which are offered elsewhere. But in the final analysis, the evidence for the existence of the good (God) is not vitiated by the anomaly of evil. Evil remains a perplexing mystery, but the force of the mystery is not enough to demand that we throw out the positive evidence for God, for the reality of good, and the reality of evil.

Key Points to Remember

Where did evil come from?

1. The question of the origin of evil has not been answered satisfactorily. We can create various kinds of explanations that may impress people with their clever character, but they all have their deficiencies. Christian truth is not served by clever sophistry.

2. When we talk about evil we tend to do it in negative terms. Even our language betrays the fact that if we even think about evil we must do it against a background of the good. Even though we may not understand the origin of evil, we recognize that the reality of evil gives indirect evidence for the existence of God.

3. While we cannot explain the existence of evil, that is no reason for us to disregard the positive evidence for God. To deny what we do know on the basis of what we don't know is not only bad theology but bad science as well. The case for the existence of God must rely on other grounds than the moral issue of good and evil.

4. Christians may not be able to explain evil, but they are exhorted to beware of the influence of evil. "Be sober, be watchful. Your adversary the devil prowls around like a roaring lion, seeking someone to devour. Resist him, firm in your faith, knowing that the same experience of suffering is required of your brotherhood throughout the world. And after you have suffered a little while, the God of all grace, who has called you to his eternal glory in Christ, will himself restore, establish, and strengthen you" (1 Pet. 5:8-10).

Note

1. Leibniz's theory of *petite perceptions* in his monadology complicates this point considerably.

nine

"Why Does God Allow Suffering?"

It was Pascal who, in the midst of his consideration of the nature of man and his concern to pinpoint his uniqueness as precisely as he could, described man as a great paradox. He said that the paradox is located in the fact that of all the creatures in this world, man is at the same time that creature of the highest grandeur and of the worst misery. He said that the focus of man's grandeur is in his capacity to reflect analytically on his own existence in a way that transcends anything we find in the animal kingdom. And yet, that very point of grandeur is at the same time man's point of misery. For as Pascal says, "He has the ability to contemplate a better existence than he presently enjoys."

At the point of contemplating a better existence than he presently enjoys, Pascal touches on the very nerve of the question of the reality of human suffering. For the striking thing is that we have the capacity at least to think about life without suffering.

Recently I heard a man read from the very last chapters of the New Testament, from the Revelation of Jesus Christ to John. They are a record of the vision that John had of the inner gates of heaven and of the New Jerusalem coming down as a bride adorned from the throne of grace. They contain a matchless description of what it will be like on the other side, where there will be no sorrow or death or pain or suffering. They tell us that God Himself will come to each of His people and personally wipe the tears away from his or her eyes forever. It is a great vision, a marvelous vision! But the tears are still with us today. And until the moment comes when our eyes are lifted up to heaven and we see the New Jerusalem coming down as a bride adorned for her husband, we will have to deal with this problem.

Why Do We Have to Suffer?

There are multiple answers to the question of suffering proffered over the years of the history of Western civilization. Indeed, every philosophical theory has to deal with it in some way. I would like to look briefly at four different approaches to the question of suffering outside Christianity and then come back and look at these same approaches through the eyes of the Christian faith. The four approaches are those I call the Docetic, the Stoic, the hedonist, and the existential. Let me define each of of them.

The Docetic approach: suffering isn't real. The Docetic approach is that found initially, as the term suggests, in the historical movement known as Docetism. It was a variety of Gnosticism which, following certain platonic tendencies, denied the full reality of the human nature of Jesus. It saw the physical world as being less than perfect and less than real. It consequently concluded that suffering belonged only to the lower order of reality. I give the term Docetism to any theory that fails to take suffering seriously.

The modern "docetist" treats suffering as an illusion. Practitioners of Christian Science, for example, deal with suffering in this way. Here the way to overcome suffering is the way of "mind over matter." Pain belongs to the physical realm which is not real. By this approach suffering is not healed, but denied.

The Stoic approach: philosophical imperturbability. Here we think of the classic school of Stoicism at that period in history when Greek philosophy had degenerated from the lofty quests of earlier schools of metaphysics to more earthly preoccupations. At this point it was dealing with questions like, "How does a person live a successful life?" Stoics as well as Epicureans were concerned primarily with "How can I live my life in this world so as to achieve peace of mind?" Both schools sought the peace of mind that goes hand in hand with having no problems.

But although the Stoics and the Epicureans had the same goal, they had radically different methods for how to achieve that goal. The Stoic method was simple. Stoics came to the conclusion that everything that takes place in the physical world happens on the basis of mechanistically determined physical causes over which we have no control. That is, there is nothing you or I can ever do, think, say or achieve that will change the course of human events.

So they said, "Since conscience, human actions, and human events are strictly determined by impersonal forces of nature and since there is nothing we can do about what happens, the only thing left to us is to control our response to what happens. It is that alone that can set me free." They said, "All of the forces of nature cannot compel me to react against my will."

Thus the Stoics limited freedom to "my personal attitudes." And they said, "The way to overcome suffering is by *philosophical imperturbability*." That is, they attempted to condition their emotions to such a degree that nothing could disturb them. They tried to remain calm no matter what happened. This view has survived to our own day, when we speak of people who maintain a "stoic" attitude toward problems.

The Hedonistic approach: pain and pleasure. The Hedonistic approach also has its roots in antiquity. It is associated with the Epicureans, for although it antedates them, the Epicureans nevertheless refined the earlier and grosser forms of hedonism by seeking to establish an equilibrium between pleasure and pain. Their basic principle was that when we experience pain we are to balance the suffering by pleasure. Thus, if one is suffering too much, the answer to the suffering is to go out and increase the amount of pleasure. This approach to the problem of suffering is escapist. It seeks to intoxicate one's self from the full force of the suffering by overwhelming the suffering with other feelings.

The Existential approach: life is absurd. I am thinking of existentialism here in terms of the most radical variety of atheistic existentialism which maintains that there are no ultimate values and no ultimate meaning to human existence. I think of Nietzsche as one representative of this viewpoint. Nietzsche believed that life is ultimately meaningless. Nevertheless, since we are still faced with the daily question of how to live in a world of suffering, Nietzsche advocated the principle of "dialectic courage." Dialectic courage is the courage that exists in the context of the tension of meaninglessness and of absurdity. It is telling people, "Be of good cheer, for life is absurd." That is dialectical. The heroic man is the man who dares to build his house on the slopes of a volcano knowing that sooner or later the volcano is going to erupt and take that house crashing down.

This is the courage of a man like actor Jimmy Cagney in the old B-movies of the forties and fifties. For example, in *The White Cliffs of Dover*, Cagney stood against all the orders of authority and dared things that no one else dared. In the final scene of the movie, Cagney steered his single-engine plane, in flames, right into the side of the cliffs of Dover. But just before he crashed he spit out of the cockpit into that mountain and then went down heroically in a ball of flame. That is our existential hero. He grits his teeth and faces the problem without letting it defeat him, knowing all the while that even the teeth-gritting will not solve it.

We think of a more recent film entitled *They Shoot Horses, Don't They?* The Nietzschean theme is expressed in the marathon dance motif of the movie, where the contestants dance on and on and on, and one by one they drop into exhaustion or death by heart attack while the fiendish master of ceremonies sits at his little desk exploiting them. They are trying to persevere for a prize they have forgotten about since they entered the contest, but he urges them on, saying, "Yowsa, yowsa, yowsa! Look at those kids go! 'Round and 'round and 'round!" There is no end to the suffering until someone has the grace to put one of the contestants out of her misery by blowing her brains out. And when they come to this person and ask why he has done it, he can only reply, "They shoot horses, don't they?"

Albert Camus looks at the problem of suffering and says that the only ultimate philosophical question is the question of suicide. Thus, like Shakespeare's *Hamlet*, the existentialist looks at the problem and raises the question:

> To be, or not to be; that is the question;
> Whether 'tis nobler in the mind to suffer
> The slings and arrows of outrageous fortune,
> Or to take arms against a sea of troubles,
> And by opposing end them.

That is the question the existentialist faces every day of his life.

These are some of the approaches to the problem of suffering that are offered to modern man. But how do they differ from the biblical approach to suffering?

What Does the Bible Say About Suffering?

With respect to Docetism, the Christian says categorically and unequivocally, "We refuse to look at suffering as illusion." At the heart of the biblical revelation is a very earnest assertion of the stark reality of suffering in this world. There is no attempt to hide it or gloss it over. The Bible simply does not attempt to deal with the problem of suffering by euphemism.

All doctors are given to euphemisms. You go to a dentist with a toothache, for example. He takes out some ghastly instrument of Chinese torture and tells you to "open wide." You know what is coming, but he says, gently, "Now this may cause a bit of discomfort." The word "discomfort" is a euphemism. What he means is, "It's going to hurt. It's going to make you suffer." We all use euphemism like that. Preachers do. We tell people that they had better be careful or they are going to face eternal separation from God. That is a euphemism. By contrast, the Bible acknowledges the stark reality of hell and speaks of it clearly.

Novelist Herman Melville recognized reality in his own struggles with his Christian heritage and with his family. In *Redburn* he said, "Until we understand that one grief outweighs a thousand joys, we will never understand what Christianity is all about." At that point he sounds like the Old Testament writer who says, "It is better to go to the house of mourning than to spend your time with fools" (see Eccl. 7:2). Notice that our Saviour was "a man of sorrows, and acquainted with grief" (Isa. 53:3). He was the suffering servant of Israel. There is no attempt to hide this, no attempt to gloss it over. Nor, by contrast is there any attempt to glorify it or wallow in it. Rather, suffering is simply recognized as a part of the experience of every human being. We are creatures of suffering. Our way is the *via dolorosa*, the road of sorrow or grief.

Unfortunately, the Docetic approach to suffering has infiltrated parts of the Christian church. There are those, even in evangelical circles, who think that there is something wrong about acknowledging the reality of suffering in this world and who act in all piety as if it did not exist.

What about the Stoic approach? Christians are not called to be Stoics. As the people of God, we do not seek imperturbability. The Stoic mentality has, nevertheless, influenced the Christian community, and so many times people have confused Christianity and Stoicism as if it were a Christian duty never to experience grief or never to allow oneself to feel the passionate suffering.

Like so many Bildads and Eliphazes (see Job 2:11), Christian friends surround us in the midst of pain and suffering saying, "Keep a stiff upper lip." But a stiff upper lip is for Stoics, not Christians. Rather than this, Jesus comes to the tomb of Lazarus and weeps. In the Old Testament, saints of God rend their garments and wail. In fact, the lament is an inspired literary form of Scripture.

There is no sin in grief. There is a difference between grief and bitterness, sorrow and hostility. So while we are not to be bitter, we are nevertheless allowed to experience grief. There is a time to cry, as well as a time to dance (see Eccl. 3:1-9). There is a time to experience pain and cry out to God in the midst of that pain. The Bible is filled with the records of the heroes of the people of God whose pillows are wet from their tears. Jesus made the statement "Blessed are those who mourn" (Matt. 5:4). There may be a sense in the Sermon on the Mount in which Jesus is talking about mourning for our sin, but that is not all He is talking about. Jesus is talking about the basic experience of mourning.

We do not believe in a kind of determinism that says that suffering is something over which we have no control. The theme song of the church is not "Que Será Será," whatever will be will be.

What about the hedonistic approach? Should we drown our sorrows by heaping up pleasures? We can find intrusions of this theme here and there in Christian circles. Martin Luther wrote on one occasion that when he became depressed he sometimes found that the best solution (though he put in parenthesis, "I do not recommend this to other people") was to go out and have a drinking bout. Well, that is Luther! Luther can handle it. But I am glad he wrote the parenthesis, because it is bad advice to tell the people of God to seek a solution to suffering through intoxication.

In the final analysis, every hedonist has to face the hedonistic paradox that the more pleasure he experiences, the more frustrated he becomes and the more aware he is of the reality of his suffering.

Sin and suffering. What about the existential approach? Perhaps it is this one, more than any other, that makes us eager to respond as Christian people and gives

137

us a forum from which to speak about the reality of God's sovereignty. Our answer to the existentialist must start with his nihilism. As Christians we can never see suffering as meaningless. We see an undeniable relationship between the reality of suffering and the reality of sin, but at this point we must proceed very cautiously. We note that there is no suffering before the fall. We note also that in the new heaven and earth, where there is no sin, there is also no suffering. Suffering is linked to sin. At the same time, we must never establish a simple one-to-one equation between a person's suffering and his sin.

This is part of the lesson of the ninth chapter of the Gospel of John. When Jesus healed the blind man the disciples asked Jesus, "Why was this man born blind? Was it for his sin or the sin of his father?" Jesus said, "Both of your alternatives are wrong. It was not for this man's sin nor for the sin of his father that he was born blind, but that God might be glorified." Notice that Jesus does not concede that the man's blindness is a direct result of retributive justice. Nor does He say, "It just happened." Rather, there was a reason for it, but that reason was not part of an equation involving his sin. It is the same with Job. When Job suffered as he did, his friends came to him and said, "Job, you have a lot of repenting to do. Anybody suffering this much must be really wicked." But they missed the whole point.

On the other hand, we dare not jump to conclusions in the other direction and say that there is never a relationship between human suffering and the corrective wrath of God. Anytime I suffer I should ask: What does God have in mind? He may not have anything in mind that I will ever know about in this world. But He might, because we know that the Scriptures teach us that God does chastise those whom He loves and that part of the chastening process is the experience of pain and suffering. I may not come to the conclusion that my particular pain at a particular moment is for a particular sin. But I should certainly allow the occasion of my suffering to be at the same time an occasion for an evaluation of my relationship to God.

The wrong question. We see this matter of sin and suffering handled in a particularly astonishing way when another question was put to Jesus. On this occasion some people had come to Jesus and said, "What about those 18 people who were killed when the tower of Siloam fell over on them and crushed them? And what about the Galileans who were killed at the very moment of making their offerings?" (see Luke 13:1-5). These 18 people were presumably walking down the street, minding their own business. They were not heckling the construction workers. They were not blaspheming. They were just walking down the street, and the tower fell on their heads and they were crushed.

How did Jesus answer? Did He say, "I know that the Old Testament says, 'He who keepeth Israel neither slumbers nor sleeps,' but you have to understand that this is Hebrew poetry and that the Jewish people of the Old Testament are given to hyperbole. Remember that my Father gets tired. We read in the opening chapters of Genesis that He created heaven and earth in six days and finally took a rest. I suppose that on this particular afternoon He was just taking his 40 winks and the tower accidentally fell over on the heads of these people. I promise I'll communicate with my Father. I'll ask Him to be more efficient in the future." Is that what Jesus said? No, that is not what He said!

Nor did Jesus say, "I know I said that the hairs of your head are all numbered and that my Father knows every sparrow that touches the earth. But I was just trying to make a point. Don't push it too far. Remember what a herculean task it is to count all the hairs on all the heads of all the people on earth. Do you know how many birds there are in this world? Well, this one afternoon there was a great flock of migratory birds that diverted my Father's attention from that tower." That is not what He said.

What did He say? The words He gave were words that theologians put under the category of the hard sayings of Jesus. He said, "Unless you repent you will all likewise perish" (Luke 13:5). What an answer! What is Jesus saying here? I think that what He is saying is that these people were asking the wrong question. The question they should have asked is not "Why did God allow these innocent people to die by having a tower fall on their heads?" Rather, the question they should have asked is: "Jesus, why didn't that tower fall on me?" We are puzzled and bewildered whenever we see suffering in this world because we have become accustomed to the mercy and the long-suffering of God. Amazing grace is no longer amazing to us. So our astonishment is in the wrong place. The real question is: Why has God not destroyed us all since we got out of our beds this morning? Why does He tolerate us as we continue our work of sin and destruction upon His planet?

Real injustice. But you say, "Wait a minute; there is still the problem of unrequited evil, of injustice in this world." Yes! There is a very real sense in which you and I suffer unjustly in this world compared to other people. In the earlier part of the book of Revelation you have the saints of God behind the altar crying out for vindication. They had been abused. They had been slandered, persecuted. They had been slain by wicked people for righteousness' sake. We look and understand that there is such a thing as injustice. It is not an illusion. When you slander me, you have created an injustice and caused me to suffer unjustly with respect to our relationship. When I slander you I injure you without just cause. But there is a certain sense in which, although we may suffer unjustly at the hands of men, horizontally, we can never turn in the vertical direction to look into the face of the Creator and say, "God, it isn't fair!" We cannot do that because, although the horizontal relationship may be one of injustice, the vertical relationship is never one of injustice. I always tell my students, "You can pray about whatever you want to pray about, my friends; but don't ever ask for justice from God, because you might get it."

What I am saying is that the suffering of the Christian or anyone else in this world is never ultimately an accident. All suffering is within the pale of divine sovereignty. All suffering comes within the broader context of the sovereignty of God. However, when you start asking about particular cases and particular applications, we cannot answer that question.

Job wanted an answer. I think he pushed God a bit too hard when he screamed out for vindication. So when God answered Job out of the whirlwind, He said, "Who is this who darkens counsel with words without knowledge? What is your name?" As if He did not know his name! He knew his name. He knew who it was. He knew that it was His servant Job upon whom He had heaped blessing upon blessing, prosperity upon prosperity. And then He said, "Job, I'll answer your questions, after you answer mine. I'm going to interrogate you just a little bit. Job, where were you when I established the foundations of heaven and earth? Where were you, Job? What was your address?" And Job is looking at Him, his lips quivering; and he is trying to think of an answer, but he does not have time. God goes on to the next question. "Job, can you send a bird south in the winter? Can you find the lion's prey? Can you bind the stars in the sky? Can you? Can you? Can you?"

Job says, "No," chapter after chapter after chapter.

And when God is all finished Job says, "I am sorry I asked. I abhor myself. I repent in dust and ashes. I take my hand and I place it upon my mouth and speak no more" (see Job 34—42).

I think this is telling us that, although we know with certainty that all suffering fits into the scheme of God's sovereignty, nevertheless, there are those things about suffering that God has not chosen to reveal. This is where trust is really put to the test in the Christian's life. There is nothing glamorous about pain, but we have the right to ask God why. There are two ways in which we can ask that question. We can ask it angrily or calmly. If God is pleased to show us the ultimate meaning of our suffering in this life when we ask calmly, then we are blessed. But if He is pleased to wait until we see without the prism fully, then we are also blessed. Because, in this latter case, God does say certain things about suffering for us that we can live with and grasp now.

Triumph in tragedy. God tells us that in this He stands against the existentialist. He says that suffering can be redeemed, that it is not the last word. That is why no true Calvinist would ever hide behind the doctrine of God's sovereignty in the face of social responsibility to be the agents of alleviation of suffering in this world. We know that suffering can be redeemed and that we can be used of God to bring that redemption to bear. So we are to be concerned about feeding the hungry, clothing the naked, healing the sick, visiting and caring for the orphan and the widow. Ultimately we know that suffering is fully redemptive in the hands of God.

Suffering itself is used by God for our sanctification.

Asking "Why do we suffer?" is like asking the doctor, "Why do we have to take that awful tasting medicine?" Who wants an operation? Who wants to have a knife cut through the skin of our body? Nobody! But the context of suffering is sin. And part of the process of our sanctification is the crucible of suffering.

That is why Peter can say to us, "Do not think it a strange thing when you are called upon to suffer." Why should we be surprised that suffering exists in a world of sin when we see that suffering itself is used in the depths of the riches of the grace of God to bring about our very sanctification? Fire is hot, but it does refine; it produces precious gold. And the Christian faith is what Luther called a *theologia crucis*, a theology of the cross, of suffering and pain. The New Testament does not say to Christian people, "You *might* suffer." It says, "You *will* suffer" (see John 15:20-27).

Moreover, it not only says, "You *will* suffer," it says "You *must* suffer" (see Rom. 8:17). So every baptized person carries the sacramental sign of his or her participation in the humiliation of Christ. He carries the sign of his identification with the suffering servant of Israel. Yet, although our suffering is real and although our pain abides, we know that this is the way (irony of ironies) that God in His magnificent sovereignty has chosen to save the world.

We are called to courage in the midst of suffering. But our courage is not dialectical. Jesus does not come to us like some kind of existential Good Humor man who says, "Wrap up your troubles in an old kit bag and smile, smile, smile." He says, "Be of good cheer, I have overcome the world" (John 16:33). If we can accept that truth, then we can rejoice in tribulation even if we do not fully understand it. If it is not true, then we should sleep late tomorrow morning.

Key Points to Remember

Why does God allow suffering?

1. *Suffering is real and can't be dealt with piously or simplistically.* No one can tell us why we must go through suffering. The Christian must openly acknowledge the presence of the tragic in life. Any attempt to give pat answers to grief will be met with contempt.

2. *Docetism (suffering is an illusion), Stoicism (face suffering with passive acceptance), hedonism (overcome or avoid suffering by pleasure-intoxication), and existentialism (recklessly defy suffering) are inadequate approaches to suffering.* Christians must face the problem of suffering head-on.

3. *Suffering is related to sin; but people do not always suffer in direct proportion to their sin.* Suffering is a consequence of human fallenness. Suffering is a result of sin. Here it is crucial that we not make the mistake Job's friends made, to assume simplistically that every person suffers in direct proportion to his sin and guilt.

4. *The ultimate question of suffering is "Why don't we all suffer more than we do?"* We should wonder why God has not destroyed us all since we got out of our beds this morning. Why does He tolerate us as we continue our work of sin and destruction upon His planet?

5. *Christians are called to participate in the suffering of Christ.* God uses suffering as a means of redemption. Christ is the model of the Suffering Servant who triumphs over the world through the avenue of suffering. All Christians are called upon to participate in the suffering of Christ. We embrace suffering not to gain merit or to be involved in masochism but to identify with Christ's ministry to those in pain.

"When You're Dead You're Dead! There Is No More!"

Death is obscene. It runs counter to the vibrant flow of life. When we encounter it we shrink from it in horror. We use our finest cosmetics to disguise its impact. When death strikes it always leaves the question, "Is this the end?" Is there absolutely nothing more to hope for?

Perhaps the most ancient question of all is the question, "Is there life after death?" We think of Job in the throes of his misery crying out, "When a man dies, will he live again?" (see Job 14:14). We think of Hamlet musing over the question of suicide in his classic soliloquy, "To be, or not to be?" He contemplates the mystery of the grave and weighs the burdens of the alternatives of life and death. He retreats from suicide asking if man would "rather bear those ills we have than fly to others we know not of?"[1] From Job to Hamlet to the present day the question persists, "Is there life after death?"

A negative spirit of skepticism has made itself felt in the cultural atmosphere of our age. A sense of despair and hopelessness characterizes much of our culture. We hear such statements as "When you're dead, you're dead"; "This is the Pepsi generation, the now generation." The television commercial exhorts us to live our lives with gusto because we only go around once. Those who persist in their hope of a future life are regarded as weaklings who are clinging to naive superstitions that are outmoded. Christians have received their share of the scorn and ridicule for hoping in fantasies of "pie in the sky." But the issue is not simply a religious question. The issue is far more significant than that. It is the issue of the meaning of all of life. If death is ultimate then life becomes a cruel and mocking joke.

From ancient times the keenest minds of mankind have sought intellectual evidence for the survival of the soul or spirit beyond the grave. Charlatans and magicians have plied their arts couching their tricks in a garb of pseudo-intellectualism. Scholars have given the question serious attention because it is the most serious of all questions. But for the most careful and sober scholar the issue of death has strong emotional overtones. No one can face the question dispassionately for it touches each one of us in a final way.

Does Nature Teach that There Is Life After Death?

Plato faced the question in a deeply personal way when he visited his beloved mentor, Socrates, in his prison cell. As Socrates prepared himself for execution by enforced drinking of hemlock he discussed the question of immortality with his students. The Socratic argument for life after death is recorded by Plato in his famous Phaedo Dialogue.

Plato explored the question primarily from the vantage point of analogies found in nature. He detected a kind of cycle that was common to nature. He noted that spring follows winter which in turn moves inexorably toward another winter. Winter does not terminate in itself but yields again to spring. The cycle goes on as day follows night and heat follows cold. The pattern continues. He examined the drama of the germination of the seed into flowering life. For the seed to bring forth its life it must first go through a process of rotting. The shell of the seed must decay and die before the life that is locked within it can emerge. He saw here an analogy to life and death. Just as a seed must die and disintegrate before the flower emerges, so the human body must die before the life of the soul can come forth.

Plato looked beyond the realm of flowers to the animal kingdom and was stimulated by the drama of metamorphosis. The beauty of the butterfly begins in the grotesque form of the caterpillar. The caterpillar appears as a worm, bound to the earth, virtually immobile and unattractive. The worm forms for itself an insulated cocoon, withdrawing from the outside world. The cocoon remains dormant and inert for a season. In time the drama mounts as a new creature begins to scratch and stretch its way out of the cocoon. Wings and a body begin to appear and suddenly the woven prison yields a magnificent soaring creature of multicolored beauty. From the "death" of the caterpillar comes the new life of the butterfly!

These analogies from Plato do not present compelling evidence for life beyond the grave. Plato understood that they were but analogies that provide hope in the face of mystery. He was aware that butterflies do not live forever, but he pointed to the complexities of the various forms of life that surround us to cause us to move with caution in the face of unbridled skepticism.

Must We Live as If There Is a God?

In later times another philosopher approached the question from a different perspective. Immanuel Kant was perhaps the most weighty and significant philosopher of all time. Certainly his massive work has been a watershed for the development of modern thinking. Though skeptical about man's ability to prove immortality by reason alone, he offered an ingenious argument for life after death. His argument offers practical "evidence" for the existence of God and for life after death.

Kant observed that all people seem to have some concern for ethics. Though morality differs from person to person and society to society, all people wrestle with questions of right and wrong. All human beings have some sense of moral duty. Kant asked, "What would be necessary for this human sense of duty to make sense?" Are our moral senses merely the by-product of parental discipline or the imposition of society's standards? Kant thought it went deeper than that. Still the question of the origin of moral sense is different from its ultimate meaning. He noticed that we have such a sense of duty and asked what would make it meaningful? Kant answered his own question by saying that ultimately for ethics to be meaningful there must be justice. From a coldly practical perspective he asked, "Why be ethical if justice does not prevail?"

Kant saw justice as an essential ingredient for a meaningful ethic. But he noticed at the same time that justice does not always prevail in this world. He observed what countless others have also observed, that the righteous do suffer and the wicked do often prosper in this life. His practical reasoning continued by arguing that since justice does not prevail here in this world there must be a place where it does prevail. For justice to exist ultimately there must be several factors accounted for.

We must survive the grave. For there to be justice, there must be people to receive it. Since we do not receive it in this world, we must survive the grave. Justice demands life beyond death, if ethics are to be practical.

There must be a judge. Justice requires judgment and judgment requires a judge. But what must the judge be like to insure that his judgment is just? Kant answered that the judge himself must be just. If the judge is unjust then he would be prone to pervert justice rather than establish it. The judge must be utterly and completely just to insure ultimate justice. But even just judges are capable of perpetrating injustice if they make a mistake. Honest judges have convicted innocent people who were framed or surrounded by an overwhelming amount of circumstantial evidence. Our just judge must be incapable of such mistakes. To render perfect justice, he must have a perfect knowledge of all the facts and mitigating circumstances. A perfect judge must be nothing less than omniscient.

There must be judgment. A perfectly just and omniscient judge is necessary for justice but is not enough to insure it. Once the perfect judge offers his perfect verdict, the sentence must be carried out. If proper rewards and punishments are to be meted out, the judge must have the authority and the power to carry them out. If our just and omniscient judge is impotent then we have no guarantee of justice. Perhaps an evil power would prevent the judge from carrying out justice. Thus the judge would have to have perfect power of omnipotence.

Thus, for Kant, practical ethics require life after death and a judge whose description sounds very much like that of the God of Christianity. Kant recognized that his arguments were of a practical nature. He did not think that he had provided an airtight case for the existence of God or for life after death. But he did reduce the practical options for man to two. He said we have either full-bodied theism with life after death or we have no meaningful basis ultimately for our ethical decisions and actions. Without ethics life is chaos and ultimately impossible. Without God ethics are meaningless. Thus Kant's conclusion was: "We must live as though there were a God." For Kant, life was intolerable without a solid basis for ethics. If death is ultimate then no ethical mandate is really significant.

What If Life Is Meaningless?

Kant's practical optimism was not universally welcomed. The existentialists of modern culture have taken the option Kant refused. They've dared to ask the unaskable question: "What if life is meaningless?" Shakespeare's *Macbeth* says despairingly:

Life's but a walking shadow, a poor player
That struts and frets his hour upon the stage
And then is heard no more. It is a tale
Told by an idiot, full of sound and fury,
Signifying nothing.[2]

Maybe there is no justice. Maybe there is only the tale of the idiot. Perhaps life is ultimately so much sound and fury that is empty and void of significance. Why should we live as though there is a God if in fact there is no God?—These are the penetrating questions of modern man. All attempts to maintain faith in God and faith in life after death may be only exercises of wish fulfillment for those not courageous enough to face the grim facts of our sound and fury.

Ingmar Bergman states the dilemma of modern man

150

in a dialogue contained in his film *The Seventh Seal.*
Here a conversation ensues between Knight and Death:

Knight: "Do you hear me?"

Death: "Yes, I hear you."

Knight: "I want knowledge, not faith, not supposition, but knowledge. I want God to stretch out his hand towards me, to reveal himself and speak to me."

Death: "But he remains silent."

Knight: "I call out to him in the dark, but no one seems to be there."

Death: "Perhaps no one is there."

Knight: "Then life is an outrageous horror. No one can live it in the face of death knowing that all is nothing."[3]

Long before existentialism was in vogue and playwrights and novelists began to flood our nation with cries of despair, America listened to the painful poetry of Edgar Allen Poe. Some say he was brilliant; others that he was demented. Still others maintain that he was a little of both. One thing is certain; he had a unique ability to express the anguish of the human soul who experiences the loss of a loved one. His poetry is filled with the mournful groans of the bereaved. Consider his short poems such as "Annabel Lee" or "Ulalume." But it is in "The Raven" that the urgency of the issue of life after death is most clearly expressed. The poem begins:

Once upon a midnight dreary, while I pondered,
weak and weary,
Over many a quaint and curious volume of forgotten lore,
While I nodded, nearly napping
suddenly there came a tapping,
As of some one gently rapping, rapping at my
chamber door.

151

" 'Tis some visitor," I muttered, "tapping at my
  chamber door;
      Only this and nothing more."

Ah, distinctly I remember, it was in the bleak
  December,
And each separate dying ember wrought its ghost
  upon the floor.
Eagerly I wished the morrow; vainly I had sought
  to borrow
From my books surcease of sorrow, sorrow for the
  lost Lenore,
For the rare and radiant maiden whom the angels
  named Lenore,
      Nameless *here* forevermore.

In the introduction Poe sets the scene of his midnight
remorse crushed by his loneliness and the fear of the
morrow. With the appearance of his nocturnal visitor
who comes from the shores of hell, the poet asks the
burning question, "Will I ever see Lenore again?" The
reply of the fiendish bird is always the same, "Nevermore." The poem moves along to the point where the
tormented man screams in anger at his visitor:

"Prophet!" said I, "thing of evil!—prophet still, if
  bird or devil!
Whether tempter sent, or whether tempest tossed
  thee here ashore,
Desolate, yet all undaunted, on this desert land
  enchanted—
On this home by horror haunted—tell me truly, I
  implore:
Is there—*is* there balm in Gilead?—tell me—tell
  me I implore."
      Quoth the raven, "Nevermore!"

And the raven, never flitting, still is sitting, *still* is
    sitting
On the pallid bust of Pallas just above my chamber
    door;
And his eyes have all the seeming of a demon's that
    is dreaming;
And the lamplight o'er him streaming throws his
    shadow on the floor;
And my soul from out that shadow that lies floating
    on the floor
      Shall be lifted—nevermore!

The poem ends in despair. No hope is given for the
future. Such an ending is intolerable for many. The current rage of occult films and deep fascination with
parapsychology are evidence of the protest of modern
man to the prophets of despair. New interest in the
recollections of people resuscitated from clinical death
have spawned hope that tangible evidence of survival
may be available from science.

What Is the Biblical Case for Life After Death?

The strongest and most cogent case for life after death
comes to us from the New Testament. At the heart of
the proclamation of the ancient Christian community is
the staggering assertion that Jesus of Nazareth has survived the grave.

Christ was resurrected from the dead. In a classic
treatment of the question of life after death, the apostle
Paul summarizes the evidence for the resurrection of
Christ in his first letter to the Corinthians. His Epistle
comes partly in response to skepticism that arises in the
Corinthian church. Note how he deals with the question:

    Now if Christ is preached as raised from the
    dead, how can some of you say there is no

resurrection of the dead? But if there is no resurrection of the dead, then Christ has not been raised (1 Cor. 15:12,13).

The logic of this assertion is almost humorously simple. If Christ is raised, then obviously there is such a thing as resurrection from the dead.

On the other hand, if there is no resurrection from the dead, then Christ cannot be raised. The question of Christ's resurrection is crucial to the entire issue of life after death. The apostle follows with an interesting line of reasoning. He considers the alternatives to the resurrection of Christ. He uses the "if-then" formula of logical progression.

If Christ has not been raised, then our preaching is in vain and your faith [also] is in vain (1 Cor. 15:14).

Paul gets to the heart of the matter quickly. If Christ is not raised then it is clear that the preaching of the early church is an exercise in futility. The preaching becomes empty words and the faith that follows is worthless.

Moreover we are even found to be false witnesses of God, because we witnessed against God that He raised Christ, whom He did not raise, if in fact the dead are not raised. For if the dead are not raised, not even Christ has been raised; and if Christ has not been raised, your faith is worthless; you are still in your sins. Then those who also have fallen asleep in Christ have perished (1 Cor. 15:15-18, *NASB*).

The implications of the Corinthians' skepticism continue. If Christ is not raised then the apostolic witness is a false one. God has been implicated in a spurious historical claim. Again Paul mentions the futility of faith

154

and adds to it the serious result that man is still without a redeemer. Then, almost as an afterthought, Paul touches the emotional nerve of his readers by reminding them of the fate of their departed loved ones. They have perished. At this point the apostle sounds a bit like the "Raven." He is saying that, without resurrection, death is final.

The madness of the concept of the finality of death came home to me in a somewhat unusual fashion. On July 1, 1965, my wife gave birth to our son. I remember the exhilarating experience of observing him through the nursery window at the hospital. All of the dynamism of life seemed to be captured in the animated action of this newborn child. I was thrilled to behold one who was "flesh of my flesh and bone of my bone." I experienced the inordinate pride that so often attends fatherhood.

The experience of birth was by no means unique or even unusual. What followed, however, was not commonplace. The first visitor to the hospital was my mother. Her delight in witnessing her grandson was unbounded. I took her home from the hospital and spent the night in her house. The following morning I went into her bedroom to awaken her for breakfast. There was no response, no movement. As I touched her hand to rouse her, I felt the chill of death. Her body was hard and cold. She had died during the night. Within the space of a few hours I witnessed the birth of my son and the corpse of my mother. As I stood stunned by her bedside, a sense of the surreal came over me. I thought, "This is absurd. A short time ago she was a living, breathing, dynamic human being, filled with warmth and vitality. Now there is only coldness and silence." Within my soul I protested, "This does not make sense."

But as Paul points out, if Christ is not raised then our loved ones have perished. The Raven has the last word.

Paul continues his discourse by saying, "If we have only hope in Christ in this life, we are of all men most to be pitied" (1 Cor. 15:19, *NASB*).

Perhaps you are not a Christian. Maybe Christians tend to annoy you. Perhaps you become angry when Christians try to force their religion upon you. But if you do not believe that Christ has been raised, don't be angry with poor deluded Christians. Pity them. They have put all their eggs in a basket that cannot hold any eggs. If all the Christian has is hope with no historical reality to undergird that hope, he is committed to a life of futility. Christians need your sympathy, not your hostility.

Paul concludes his exercise in "what if" thinking by saying, "If the dead are not raised, 'Let us eat and drink, for tomorrow we die'" (1 Cor. 15:32). No resurrection? Then we may as well sleep in tomorrow. Eat, drink, be merry while you can. Get your gusto now before it's too late.

There is a striking similarity between the way the apostle Paul approaches life after death and the approach of Kant. Both are keenly aware of the grim alternatives to life after death. However, Paul does not leave us where Kant does. Kant reduces the options to two and then encourages us to choose the more optimistic one. Paul examines the grim alternatives to resurrection but does not build his case on those frightening options. Rather he says:

> For I delivered to you as of first importance
> what I also received, that Christ died for our
> sins in accordance with the scriptures, that he
> was buried, that he was raised on the third day
> in accordance with the scriptures, and that he
> appeared to Cephas, then to the twelve. Then
> he appeared to more than five hundred breth-

ren at one time, most of whom are still alive, though some have fallen asleep. Then he appeared to James, then to all the apostles. Last of all, as to one untimely born, he appeared also to me (1 Cor. 15:3-8).

Now Paul speaks in a fashion that moves beyond speculation. He doesn't play with the occult or rest his case on analogies drawn from nature. He offers two kinds of evidence. First, he appeals to the prophetic predictions of the Old Testament Scripture that are fulfilled with uncanny accuracy in the person of Christ. Secondly, he offers the testimony of numerous eyewitnesses to the event. Christ does not appear on one occasion to a secret audience, but manifests Himself on several different occasions. One occasion involves an audience of over 500 persons. Paul's final appeal is that he beheld the risen Christ with his own eyes. As John remarks elsewhere, "We declare to you what we see with our eyes and hear with our ears" (see 1 John 1:1-3). Paul then rehearses the history of his personal life following his sight of the risen Christ. He speaks of his trials, his imprisonments, his labors, all of which give credence to the impact his visual experience of the resurrected Jesus had on him.

The best argument for life after death is the record of history. The act of resurrection is as well attested to as any event from antiquity. Those who deny it do so invariably from the perspective of a philosophy that would rule the evidence out arbitrarily. Jesus Himself predicted it and spoke in an authoritative way concerning our own future life. He said, "In my father's house are many mansions. I go to prepare a place for you. If it were not so I would have told you" (see John 14:2). For those who think Christ credible, His words are overpowering. "If it were not so—" Jesus is saying in this discourse that had His disciples believed in an empty hope for the future, Jesus would not hesitate to correct it. The victorious implications of Christ's resurrection are summarized by Paul:

> Lo! I tell you a mystery. We shall not all sleep,
> but we shall all be changed, in a moment, in
> the twinkling of an eye, at the last trumpet.
> For the trumpet will sound, and the dead will
> be raised imperishable, and we shall be
> changed. For this perishable nature must put
> on the imperishable, and this mortal nature
> must put on immortality. When the perishable
> puts on the imperishable, and the mortal puts
> on immortality, then shall come to pass the
> saying that is written: "Death is swallowed up
> in victory. O death, where is thy victory? O
> death, where is thy sting?" The sting of death
> is sin, and the power of sin is the law (1 Cor.
> 15:51-56).

The triumphant summary ends with a sober conclusion:

> Therefore, my beloved brethren, be steadfast,
> immovable, always abounding in the work of
> the Lord, knowing that in the Lord your labor
> is not in vain (1 Cor. 15:58).

Your labor is not in vain. That is the essence of the New Testament message. Death is not ultimate. The answer of the Raven is "Nevermore." The answer of Christ is "Forevermore."

Key Points to Remember

Is there life after death?

1. Nature, as Plato suggests, offers analogies that give evidence and hope for future life.

2. Kant argued for life after death out of a practical concern for ethics. His argument says that universal moral sense would be meaningless apart from ultimate justice: we must survive the grave; there must be a judge; there must be judgment.

3. *If death is final then life has no ultimate meaning.* How we deal with the question of death will reveal how seriously we regard life. Existentialism and the poetry of Poe illustrate man's sense of hopelessness and futility.

4. *The Bible definitely says, "Yes, there is life after death."* Without Christ, men are without hope. Jesus said, "I am the resurrection and the life; he who believes in me, though he die, yet shall he live" (John 11:25).

5. *The biblical claim for life after death rests on credible eyewitness testimony of historical event.* The eyewitnesses were men whose work reflects sober judgment, whose contemporaries offered to refutation and whose conviction of the truth of their testimony made them willing to die for it.

6. *The ongoing power of Christ to transform human lives gives corroborative evidence to the assertion that He lives in a more real and powerful way than as an inspiring memory.*

Notes

1. *Hamlet*, act 3, sc. 1.
2. *Macbeth*, act 5, sc. 5.
3. Taken from Donald J. Drew, *Images of Man: A Critique of the Contemporary Cinema* (Downers Grove, IL: Inter-Varsity Christian Fellowship, 1974, p. 72. Used by permission.

bibliography

Beardslee, William A. *Literary Criticism of the New Testament.* Philadelphia: Fortress Press, 1970.

Bright, John. *The Authority of the Old Testament.* Grand Rapids: Baker Books, 1975.

Bruce, F.F. *The Defense of the Gospel in the New Testament.* Grand Rapids: Eerdmans, 1959.

_____. *The New Testament Documents: Are they Reliable?* Chicago: Inter-Varsity Press, 1960.

Harrison, R.K. *Introduction to the Old Testament.* Grand Rapids: Eerdmans, 1969.

Martin, James. *The Reliability of the Gospels.* London: Hodder and Stoughton, 1959.

Montgomery, John Warwick, ed. *God's Inerrant Word.* Minneapolis: Bethany Fellowship, 1974.

Orr, James. *The Bible Under Trial.* London: Marshall Brothers, n.d.

_____. *Revelation and Inspiration.* Grand Rapids: Baker Book House, 1969 (reprint).

Packer, J.I. *"Fundamentalism" and the Word of God.* Grand Rapids: Eerdmans, 1958.

Pinnock, Clark H. *Biblical Revelation.* Chicago: Moody Press, 1971.

Shelton, John H., ed. *Scripture and Confession.* Nutley, N.J: Presbyterian and Reformed Publishing Co., 1973.

Sproul, R.C. *Knowing Scripture.* Downers Grove, Illinois: Inter-Varsity Press, 1977.

Walvoord, John N., ed. *Inspiration and Interpretation.* Grand Rapids: Eerdmans, 1974.

Warfield, Benjamin B. *The Inspiration and Authority of the Bible.* Philadelphia: Presbyterian and Reformed Publishing Co., 1948.

Young, Edward J. *Thy Word Is Truth.* Grand Rapids: Eerdmans, 1957.